Awake from
DARKNESS

Awake from DARKNESS

A Memoir of Love and Survival

Tom & Mary Parker

Contents

Dedicated to all who are
walking through the storms of life.

Introduction

This is a true story.
The names have been changed.

This is the deeply personal memoir of a woman who woke from a coma with her mind lost in a fog.

My wife Mary and I tell this story as faithfully as memory allows, each sharing our own journey—each offering a truth only we could know. The story spans a ten-year period in our marriage, beginning with Mary's near-death experience. It reveals a love upended by crisis, lifted by hope, and reshaped into something new.

Our relationship began with a spark of admiration, and it grew into a love that was the foundation of our marriage. Together, we built a life filled with the gentle rhythm of shared routines and the everyday music of our children's voices. It wasn't a flashy life, but it was ours, and Mary was the heart of it. A loving wife and mother, she had laughter in her eyes and warmth in her smile, and our days were steady. Little did we know, our life was about to be shattered by an unexpected twist of fate.

In an instant, the world we had carefully built vanished. Mary sustained a brain injury that hurled us into a reality we could never have imagined—her memory of everything was gone. Herself, me, our children, every holiday we had shared, every argument, every kiss, all wiped away as if none of it had ever been.

The story of her life had turned a page to something unknown. We found ourselves struggling down a path of relentless hardship, through the darkest of days, fighting with everything we had to reclaim our lives. And almost imperceptibly, glimmers of victory started to emerge. Then Mary began to fall in love all over again—as if for the very first time.

This isn't simply the story of a woman who lost her memory. It's also the story of a couple torn apart and how they found their way back to each other when all seemed lost. It's about the spirit of endurance and the triumph of love.

Above all, this is a love story.

It is during our darkest moments that we must focus to see the light.
—Aristotle

Prologue

BANG! My car spinning—gripping the wheel—no control—rolling—slam—helpless—crashing—

Then ... silence.

No feeling. No sense of being. Nothing.

The next moment, I found myself moving down a hallway I'd never seen. Peace and love filled me, and I knew I was somewhere special. A bright light at the end of the hall drew me forward, warm and inviting, and as I stepped into it, love enveloped me.

And standing before me were two figures.

1

A Golden Morning

The day our lives would change forever began like any other. It was a golden Thursday morning in Atlanta, the kind of day that seemed filled with promise.

Mary and I lived just north of the city in a brick house tucked beside a peaceful lake, where tall trees dotted the shoreline. It was a place where our children's laughter once filled the air. Now, it was just the two of us, with a love that had only deepened through the years.

Every morning, we lingered over hot mugs of coffee and a simple breakfast, savoring time together before our jobs pulled us in different directions. I liked my coffee black, while Mary, on the other hand, swirled in cream like it was an art form. During coffee time, words were optional—just being together was enough. Sometimes we talked about the day ahead, laughing softly, the affection between us warm and easy. After thirteen years of marriage, our life felt steady and secure as if nothing could ever shake it.

Mary hummed softly as she prepared breakfast, and my thoughts turned to our vacation plan—a long weekend in Gatlinburg, Tennessee. We'd been there twice before. I was drawn to the slower, quieter pace of life, and Mary loved getting lost in the charm of the little shops.

"How long until Labor Day weekend?" I asked.

She caught my gaze and grinned, as if she'd been waiting for me to ask. "Three weeks and counting."

I smiled back. "Three weeks too long."

Her eyes softened. "How does time go by so fast?" she murmured, her voice tinged with nostalgia. "It feels like only yesterday Cody was just a little boy, running through the house, and now he's about to get married."

She paused for a moment. "He and Beth are calling tonight to talk about a venue they're visiting this weekend. They need to choose a location soon, before they miss out."

Mary and I valued family as much as our work, and we had a close relationship with our children.

"They're lucky to have your help," I said with a smile. "You make everything easier for them." I chuckled softly as I stood, gathering my breakfast dishes. "And Cody really loves having you involved, you know?"

As I carried my dishes into the kitchen, a smile tugged at my lips. Mary's face always lit up when she talked about the wedding. Her eyes sparkled, and her voice brimmed with excitement, as if every detail were a secret she couldn't wait to share.

"Darling, I'll be working a little late tonight and won't be home till about 6:30. Dinner date on the couch?"

She smiled and picked up her purse. "Sounds good. I'll get dinner from the grocery on the way home. I've recorded *America's Got Talent*. Let's watch it."

"Okay," I said, my heart warming at the thought of our quiet evening together. "I love you."

"Love you too."

I kissed her goodbye.

2

An Unfinished Life

I unlocked the front door of Dr. Jim Smith's Family Dentistry, dropped the keys into my purse, and turned on the lights. I always arrived early to prepare the office in the silence before my coworkers arrived. The morning would shift into the easy conversation and camaraderie our team shared before the rush started—when the phone began ringing, patients arrived, and the waiting room filled with voices.

Our office specialized in general dentistry and I loved my job as a dental assistant, working on the front lines of interacting with patients, elbow-deep in the rhythm of it all. And it was important work. We helped people, and to me, that was everything.

I slid my purse into a cabinet, then paused in front of the mirror on the wall for a quick check before the day kicked into high gear. Long lashes ringed dark brown eyes behind tortoiseshell glasses, and a hint of blush softened the light freckles across my cheeks. My wavy blonde hair lightly touched my shoulders. I smiled briefly, then glanced around the waiting room.

Everything was ready. Cozy furniture in place. Magazines fanned out just right.

At the reception desk, I flipped open the daily schedule book to review it, then I headed to the two treatment rooms to ensure they were prepared. The dental team called each one an operatory. The instrument trays were both set up, with everything laid out in proper position.

I was halfway back to the reception desk, to pull the patient charts for Jim and the two hygienists, when the front door swung open again. Ellen, another dental assistant, and my best friend, stepped inside.

I noticed the pink scrubs she'd chosen were nearly the same shade as mine and we almost looked like twins. She'd been with Jim for twenty years, much longer than my twelve. Old-school in her approach, there were certain things she couldn't do, like take X-rays and read them, but that wasn't a problem since, as a registered assistant, I had that covered.

She smiled when she saw me. "Good morning, Mary." She nodded back toward the door. "Looks like another hot day out there."

"Good morning," I said, returning her smile. "Yes, it does."

She set her purse beside mine in the cabinet, the familiar sound filling the moment. "How's Tom doing?"

"He's good," I replied, a warmth rising through me as I thought of him—tall, with brown hair, hazel eyes, a charming smile, a sense of humor that matched mine, and a quiet tenderness he showed only to me.

Even after all our years together, I still loved thinking about him.

I pulled my thoughts back to the job. "We've got a full day ahead, and everything's ready for the first appointment."

The front door opened again, and a thin man stepped through, his silver hair neatly combed.

"Mr. Collins!" I said in surprise.

I recognized a lot of our patients by sight, even after just a visit or two. My coworkers often commented on how good my memory was.

"I didn't see you on the schedule for today," I said, keeping my voice light, as my mind raced through the day's appointments.

He touched his jaw gingerly and mumbled, "I woke up this morning with a bad toothache."

"Well, come on in," I said, smiling. "Let's get you into a room and see what's going on."

I led him down the hall to an operatory, and he settled into the dental chair, moving slowly, while I pulled on a pair of gloves. Looking in his mouth, I quickly identified tooth number thirty-one as the culprit.

"I need to take an X-ray so we can see this tooth better," I said.

It took only a few minutes to complete the scan, and when it was done, I examined it, then pointed.

"Mr. Collins, see that dark spot right there?" I asked.

"Yeah. What's that?"

"That's a swelling at the root of the tooth. You need an endodontist. I can recommend one if you'd like, and I can call and find out if they can see you today."

After scheduling Mr. Collins for later that day, I handed him a written referral and collected the payment for the X-ray. He gave me a grateful smile, offered a quick thanks, and then he was gone.

As I cleaned the operatory to prepare it for the next patient, Jim arrived at the office, and a minute later, he stepped into the room I was cleaning.

"Good morning, Mary. How's our day look?" he asked.

"Busy," I said with a grin. "Just the way I like it."

He nodded. "I need you to call the lab and check on Terry Campbell's crown."

"I already did. It'll be delivered tomorrow. Terry's coming back on Wednesday."

"You're always on top of things," he said.

"Thanks," I replied.

It was a typical day at the office, and I moved through it with practiced ease. Soft music played in the background, mingling with the faint murmur of voices to create a rhythm that accompanied my work. Between assisting Jim with patients, I updated medical charts, made calls about insurance claims, and typed office correspondence. Each task was a thread in the fabric of my day, and I handled every chart, call, and letter with care.

As I worked, my thoughts drifted past the hum of the office and landed on Tom. I couldn't help but smile. When he had walked up to me all those years ago and said hello, I never imagined that moment would unfold into a lifetime of love.

It was the little things I enjoyed most. Our daily banter and routines. How he liked giving me flowers from the grocery store—cheerful bundles of whatever caught his eye. Daisies, carnations, sometimes sprigs of eucalyptus or baby's breath. Simple gifts that said, "I love you," and that I loved arranging in vases.

The hours of the day slipped by, and at 5:00, I exchanged quick goodbyes with my coworkers, my thoughts already on the comfort of Tom's company. I crossed the parking lot as the sun sank low, the air thick with lingering heat as though the day itself was reluctant to end.

As I drove toward home, rush-hour traffic surging around me, my thoughts turned to dinner. I planned to make Tom's favorite, Chicken Delight, a casserole he never tired of. Cooking for him was always fun, and sometimes we'd cook together.

I turned onto Highway 400, keeping a careful eye on the other vehicles as I merged into the flow of traffic, moving at fifty-five miles an hour. I cast a quick glance at the rear-view mirror and—

BANG! My car spinning—gripping the wheel—no control—rolling—slam—helpless—crashing—

Then ... silence.

No feeling. No sense of being. Nothing.

The next moment, I found myself moving down a hallway I'd never seen. Peace and love filled me, and I knew I was somewhere special. A bright light at the end of the hall drew me forward, warm and inviting, and as I stepped into it, love enveloped me.

And standing before me were two figures.

My dad and Jesus, wow!

A rush of joy welled up inside me—Dad had been gone for seven long years and seeing him again filled me with warmth.

"Daddy, I'm coming to be with you."

He shook his head slowly. "You can't. It's not your time."

"But I want to be here."

"No, not until the time is right."

I looked at Jesus. "I want to be in heaven."

He spoke to me.

"I don't understand."

"You will," he said.

3

Into the Abyss

"Hey, Tom," Mike said from my office doorway, his voice casual but curious. "Got any plans this weekend?"

"Taking Mary out to dinner," I said with a chuckle. Every weekend, without fail, I asked her out on a dinner date, as if it was the first time I'd ever asked her out.

Mike smiled and nodded. He wasn't just my boss, he was a good friend who knew I adored Mary.

Sprint's corporate office always buzzed with energy, and I enjoyed my job. I was a telecommunications manager for the eastern half of the country, one of many managers responsible for resolving the inevitable communication problems that occurred daily in Sprint's fiber optic network. When there was a problem the Sprint technicians couldn't fix, and there often was, I got an urgent call and responded quickly, sending engineers to replace equipment and solve the problem fast. Once the engineers were sent, that problem got fixed, and I was on to the next. The accounts I handled were Fortune

500 companies, hospitals, universities, and other large institutions, and they depended on me.

After a long day at work, I headed toward home, expecting a quiet evening of watching TV on the couch with Mary. I pulled into our garage at 6:25 and saw that her car was missing.

She must still be at the grocery.

Inside the house, I pulled out my phone, turned it on, and called Mary.

"Hello?"

It wasn't Mary. A jolt shot through me. I tried to place the voice, even as I knew something was very wrong.

"Lorraine?" I said slowly, my grip tightening on the phone. "This is Tom. Can I talk to Mary?"

Her reply came fast, words rushed.

"Oh, Tom! Mary was in a car accident! I tried calling you, but it went straight to voicemail. We're at the hospital an—"

"WHAT?"

"They don't know if she's going to make it—"

I cut her off, my voice sharp. "Which hospital?" Then, "I'm on my way."

I bolted for the car. Throwing caution aside, I gunned the engine and raced down the road. The four-way intersection rushed at me, the traffic light glaring red. *No time to wait!* I barely slowed, just enough to glance both directions, then swung left through the light and raced on.

God please watch over Mary.

Realizing she might be hanging on by a thread, I gripped the wheel tighter and drove even faster.

At the ER, I slammed the car into park and ran inside.

"My wife is Mary Parker," I told the admissions attendant. "And—"

Her eyes widened. "Oh, yes—" She sprang to her feet.

"—she was in a car accident. I was told she might not make it—where is she?"

"Mr. Parker! Come through here!"

She flung open a side door, waving me inside.

"Down this hall"—she pointed—"straight to the end! Hurry! Ask someone at that desk to take you to her!"

I raced down the empty white hallway, the sharp bite of antiseptic cutting through the air. My steps pounded the tile, echoing off the walls. Dread tore at me.

Nearing a nursing station, I slowed, scanning the area. People in scrubs moved about quickly. A white information board on one wall listed patient names, room numbers, and other details. Too rushed to read it, I stopped a nurse to get directions.

She smiled. "How can I help you, sir?"

"I need to find my wife. Mary Parker."

Her eyes flickered and she started stammering—unable to speak.

A tall man in a white coat rushed over. "Mr. Parker, I'm Dr. Williams. Your wife is badly hurt. We don't know if she's going to make it. Follow me."

We hurried down another hallway, both of us silent. He turned at a doorway and entered a room. I stepped in after him. And my world shattered.

She's lying on a stretcher ... motionless ... head and face bloody ... eyes closed ... clothing mostly gone ...

I stared in shock—

... black skin all around her eyes, like a raccoon's mask ... tubes and wires crisscross her body ... she's on a ventilator ... a sheet bunched at her feet ... medical wrappers and debris lay everywhere ... it looks like a war zone!

My throat constricted. "Is she alive?" I barely whispered. *No—this can't be happening.*

Dr. Williams nodded slowly. "Yes. For now."

He hesitated. "We had to shock her heart three times to keep her alive."

"Why isn't she moving?"

"She hit her head and she's in a coma."

"Will she wake up?"

The doctor looked at me with sympathy. "We don't know. The nurse will take you to a private room, Mr. Parker—while we move your wife to the Intensive Care Unit."

The nurse at Mary's bedside led me to a small room. I sat alone. Devastated. Agonizing. Waiting.

A little later she returned, her face somber. "Mr. Parker," she said gravely, "you can see your wife now. I'll take you to her room."

My mind raced as I followed her.

How can this happen to Mary? Is her brain motionless too? Can she think?

Then I saw Mary again—still in the coma and on the ventilator, tucked into crisp white sheets, wearing a hospital gown, her head wrapped in a white bandage. She looked impossibly fragile.

Doctors hurried in and out of her room, their faces tight with concern. They couldn't say how badly she was hurt.

Why not? How can I help her if they can't say what's wrong? How hurt is she?

My heart and head hurting, I prayed again and again— *God please help Mary. Please don't take her.*

The thought of losing her was unbearable, and my mind reeled.

Dylan and Cody—my two youngest stepsons, twenty-one and twenty—stepped in. Eyes wide. Faces pale. Shaken.

I hugged them tight, trying to give them a sense of reassurance I didn't feel.

They fired questions at me.

"What happened?"

"She was in a car accident."

"How hurt is she?"

"I don't know."

"Will she be okay?"

"I don't know. The doctors are trying to help her."

I told them all I knew. Not nearly enough.

As they stared at their mom, I saw the disbelief in their eyes—matching mine.

No overnight visitors were allowed in the ICU, and a nurse led me and the boys to a waiting room. Lorraine and her husband were there, though only briefly. Mary's relationship with her was distant and we didn't know them much. The boys and I sat in the empty room in shock.

God, please heal Mary and give her back to me.

Memories of Mary flooded me—her loving eyes, her smile that lit up a room, the way she cared for everyone around her, the warmth of her touch.

The boys stayed with me for two more hours, then left— still just as shaken.

Alone in the quiet room, I spent a long, sleepless night, hoping and praying Mary would survive until I could see her again.

4

Shock

First Day After the Accident

In a state of utter shock, I paced in the waiting room as morning arrived, impatient for the ICU to open.

With a heavy heart, I made the calls I didn't want to make. Mary's mom, her boss, my boss, and then my dad—delivering the devastating news. Forced by each call to face impossible questions. When asked about Mary, I could only say she was in a coma. All the calls were short.

Mike said, "Tom, take all the time you need. Don't worry about your job. Just take care of Mary."

After those calls, I headed toward Mary's room, bracing myself for what I might find.

God, please help me know how to help her.

She looked exactly the same as the night before. Her chest rose and fell with the rhythm of the ventilator. A beeping monitor tracked her heart rate.

I sat down by the bed and gently put my hand over hers.

"I'm here darling, and I'm not going anywhere," I said softly.

A man in blue scrubs and steel-rimmed glasses stepped into the room.

"Good morning, Mr. Parker. I'm Dr. Baxter, and I'm the attending physician."

"What does that mean?" I asked, standing up.

"I oversee the other doctors."

I asked him every question I could think of, aching for information. He said Mary's coma had been medically induced to stabilize her.

"Does that mean she'll wake up when the medicine wears off?" I asked.

He shook his head slowly. "There's no way to know."

My heart sank.

He studied the chart on the clipboard he held, glanced at the machines Mary was hooked to, then let his gaze settle on me.

"She's being closely monitored. We just need to be patient," he said quietly, then left the room.

Overwhelmed, I stood beside Mary, watching and waiting for what would happen next, willing her to wake.

"Mary, please, please come back to me," I whispered.

Doctors moved quickly in and out, checking on her. I questioned them, trying to understand her condition and what they planned to do. Their answers were short and provided little information.

A few family members came in briefly, murmuring words of comfort that barely registered. All I could think about was Mary.

It felt like I was inside the moment yet also watching everything from outside myself.

ON THE THIRD day, our pastor arrived and offered encouragement. I could only nod. Before he left, he prayed for us.

Watching Mary lying in the coma, it seemed as though my life had stopped.

With great reluctance, I rushed home to shower and change clothes, not wanting to be away from my sweetheart for even a moment. Each second away, anxiety twisted through me. A single minute felt like an eternity.

I need to be there when she wakes up. She has to pull through. I can't lose her.

In the shower, my tears flowed, but the moment was cut short by the urgency pulling at me.

I jumped into fresh clothes, grabbed the mail from the mailbox, dropped it on the front hall table, and rushed back to the hospital.

Mary remained motionless.

On the fourth day, her eyelids started to flutter.

5

Trapped!

Beep! Beep! Whoosh, whoosh.
Beep! Beep! Whoosh, whoosh.
Agh, that noise ... p-pain ... spinning ...
"Her eyelids are fluttering!"
... a man's v-voice ... force my eyes open ... c-can't do it ...
The man spoke again.
I'm trapped ... l-lost ... confused ...

AS MARY'S EYELIDS fluttered, a wave of relief washed
through me—*she's waking up!*
"Darling, can you hear me?" I asked.
Her eyelids stopped fluttering.
"It's good to see you awake, honey. You've been asleep for
four days."
No answer.
Gone. She's gone again.

I lowered my head into my hands.

God please, please help her.

MARY AND I were trapped in different versions of the same nightmare.

She kept drifting between unconsciousness and the edge of barely waking.

Heartbroken, I sat by her bed, watching for any change. The steady whoosh of the ventilator and the insistent beep of the heart monitor filled the air. I spoke with the medical staff as they came and went, doing whatever I could to help.

The bruises on Mary's face had turned purple and blue. As I gazed at her, memories of the first time I ever saw her flooded back.

6

The Voice of an Angel

Fourteen Years Before the Accident

I sat alone in a wooden church pew, reading the Sunday morning bulletin as I waited for the service to begin. Then piano music filled the sanctuary, and a woman's voice rose above it, clear and beautiful. It was like listening to the voice of an angel. I looked up, captivated. The longer she sang, the more I wanted the service to end so I could meet her.

When the service finally ended, I made my way toward the stage, moving against the tide of people heading in the opposite direction. My eyes quickly glanced around to find the singer before she slipped away.

Not seeing her, I asked a man standing nearby, "Do you know where the soloist went?"

He pointed to a door beside the stage. "Through there."

Stepping through the door, I saw her hanging up her choir robe, and in that moment, I realized she was even prettier up close.

"Hi," I said.

She turned to me, smiling—and when our eyes met, my heart suddenly flipped.

"I'm Tom, and your solo was beautiful."

Her smiled widened. "Thank you. I'm Mary."

The feeling of connection between us was magnetic.

The following Sunday, I spotted her at church again, and without hesitation I walked up and asked her out on a date.

She smiled. "I'd love that."

7

"It's Called a TBI"

Five Days After the Accident

Mary kept drifting in and out of consciousness, barely waking each time. Slowly, she began to wake for longer periods, but each one lasted scarcely a minute or two before she was gone again, sunk in a sleep she couldn't come out of.

Every time her eyelids fluttered, I'd lean forward, poised on the edge of the chair, hoping for her to look at me with recognition and love. But when her eyes opened, her gaze fell on me empty and lost.

She started having seizures, when asleep and awake. When awake, she passed out the moment one began. Her left arm jerked suddenly and rapidly—each seizure lasting nearly a minute. Every one of them was frightening.

Increasingly alarmed, I kept questioning the doctors.

"Mr. Parker," one of the doctors said unemotionally, "when your wife hit her head in the accident, she sustained a traumatic brain injury. It's called a TBI."

The information gripped me tightly. "Will she be okay?"

"We don't know," the doctor said.

"What happened to her brain?"

"There's no way to be sure."

"Why is she having seizures?"

"That isn't unusual after a TBI, and they should go away in time. Her seizures aren't long, and we've started her on medication to prevent them. When they happen, just watch her and make sure she doesn't get hurt. And let us know if they start lasting longer."

My mind raced, worrying how my sweetheart might be affected by the TBI.

8

The CT Scan

Six Days After

I found Dr. Baxter at the nurse's station and pressed him for more answers. "Why can't Mary wake up?"

"Mr. Parker, she was badly shaken up in the accident. You need to give her time."

"What can you tell me about her TBI?"

"It's the brain. We don't know much."

"How bad can it be?"

Dr. Baxter shook his head. "We can't say. But you need to prepare yourself. She might be cognitively impaired."

My heart plummeted. "Can you tell me anything else?"

"No. There's no way to know more until she's awake enough for us to test her. It might take her a long time to recover. We just won't know until she wakes up."

"How long will that take?"

"Mr. Parker, we don't have a lot of answers right now. As soon as we know anything, we'll tell you."

Heavyhearted, I walked to the waiting room and dropped onto the chair next to Mary's brother Joe. He was a good friend, and I needed a moment to rest and collect my thoughts.

"How are the kids handling Mary's accident?" he asked.

"I'm not sure. I've been busy with Mary and the doctors."

"That's understandable. Can I do anything to help?"

"I don't know. The doctor said we need to wait on Mary to wake up."

"Well, I'm here if you need anything."

Grateful, I told him I needed to get back to Mary.

She was asleep when I entered her room. I sat on the hard plastic chair beside her bed. Memories of our life together washed over me—the laughter, cooking side by side, cuddling on the couch in the evenings as we watched TV. Family had always been at the center of everything, and we had raised our children with love. We were active in our church. Our life had felt warm and steady.

Now, sitting in the hospital, I wondered if any of it would return.

PAIN SLOWLY PULLED me awake ...

I heard faint whispering and forced my eyes open. They slipped closed. I tried again, and peered at dim, hazy images of people.

F-fire in my head ...

Confusion spun inside me. I tried to speak. Only a breathy wheeze came out.

A blurry figure leaned over and spoke slowly.

I groaned in agony.

... fear ... lost ...

He spoke again, but nothing made sense.

I faded away.

MY HEART ACHED for my dear wife.

I leaned over and said slowly, "Mary, you can't talk. You have a tube in your throat. You're in the hospital. Are you hurting?"

She didn't respond.

"It's okay." I lightly touched her hand. "Try to relax, sweetheart. You're being taken care of. Just rest."

I didn't know if she heard me or not.

FAMILY AND FRIENDS kept calling me to check on Mary. I didn't have many answers. I asked everyone to pray for her and led the prayers over the phone.

"Father, we pray for Mary and put her into your hands. We pray for the doctors and the medical staff. Guide them in what they do. Please help Mary and take care of her. We pray for your will. Thank you. Amen."

I continued asking the doctors why Mary was having trouble waking up. She kept drifting on the edge between sleep and waking, mostly asleep.

"Give her time," they said. "We're measuring her level of consciousness and monitoring her closely. You need to be patient."

Medical staff kept moving in and out constantly, checking on Mary.

More family members came to see her, but only two visitors were allowed in the ICU at a time. I asked the head nurse to allow three so two others could come in with me, and she agreed, but the staff kept their visits few and short.

Mary was either asleep, or barely awake and extremely groggy, and didn't know who anyone was.

Seeing my sweetheart hurt so badly was crushing.

God, please help us.

Finally, Mary was taken off the ventilator, and a CT scan of her brain was ordered.

9

Our First Date

While Mary slept, I sat quietly in her room, my mind drifting back to the evening of our first date.

We had dinner at an Italian restaurant. Soft music played in the background, the smell of fresh bread and garlic filled the air, and quiet conversations drifted around the tables.

As we shared stories, we laughed easily and discovered we had a lot in common, from our likes and dislikes to our values and views on life. Both of us had been married before, and she had three young boys—nine, seven, and six—who she spoke about with pride. I told her I was a legal assistant in the U.S. Navy. She was a receptionist at a dental office. When she mentioned she'd once been a soloist for two summers with the Billy Graham Crusade, I wasn't surprised.

"I would've loved to see you on that stage," I said, grinning. "I bet you were great."

Her eyes danced in amusement as she laughed.

What a wonderful sound.

We began dating steadily. A year later, I finished my military service and took a job at a computer company as a technical support specialist. Mary completed the required courses and became a registered dental assistant. Not long after, we were married, and Mary fit into my life like the missing piece I'd always wanted.

As we juggled careers and family, we discovered we made a really good team. The boys' biological father wasn't in the picture, and from day one, I adopted them in my heart as if they were my own. Mary and I loved raising them together. We both took evening classes to sharpen our skills—computer technology for me, new dental procedures for her. It wasn't easy, but we were building something lasting, and together, we made it work.

The years rolled by, and our life settled into a steady rhythm, a fulfilling blend of careers, school events, family activities, and church. I locked in as a manager at Sprint, while Mary thrived in her role as a dental assistant. She worked in a high-volume practice, admired by both her coworkers and patients. She also became a certified member of the Georgia Forensics Dental Team, volunteering on occasional weekends.

Our life before the accident had been good, everything going according to plan. But now, all of that fell into the background of my mind.

Only one thing felt certain: Mary just had to get better.

I couldn't imagine a life without her.

10

Confusion

Eight Days After

Slowly, I drifted awake.

Head p-pounding ... agony ...

"Hey, darling," a man nearby said softly.

"W-where am I?" I whispered.

"You ... hospital."

"Wh-what?"

"It's okay, Mary. Just rest."

"B-but where ..."

"I just told you. You're in ... hospital."

"I c-can't remember ..."

"You were ... accident. You hit your head," he said.

What?

Sleep pulled at me, and I disappeared.

I WATCHED MARY'S eyes open again, and leaning close, I gently moved a loose strand of hair from her face.

"Darling, I said slowly, "do you remember my sister, Anna, came to see you today?"

No reply.

"She brought you those flowers," I added, pointing to a colorful arrangement in front of the window. "She's so sorry about your accident."

Mary's lips parted slightly. "Uh ..."

"And my dad called," I went on, "and said to tell you he loves you. He's coming to see you again tomorrow."

Seeing the confusion in her eyes, comprehension missing, sadness filled me. I smiled gently at her and took her hand.

"Is there anything I can do for you?" I asked.

Her eyes closed, and she was gone.

AWARENESS FLICKERED ...

A storm of fear and frustration swirled inside me.

I looked around.

I was alone.

In a strange bed.

A strange room.

W-where am I?

Did someone say I h-hit my head?

I reached up and felt a bandage.

What's happening?

Wait—what was I thinking?

Why d-don't I remember anything?

Lost, anguished, afraid, I passed out.

I OPENED MY eyes and saw a man sitting by my bed, holding my hand.

"W-where am I?"

"Darling, you're in ... hospital."

"What?"

"Everything's okay—"

"W-why can't I remember?"

"Do you remember anything?"

"N-no."

"You had an accident—"

"I don't ..."

"Honey, you're okay. Just rest."

"How, in—cuh—UGHH!"

What's wrong with me ...

"It's all right," he said. "Take your time. Try again."

"I—um ..." Frustration exploded inside me. *I feel horrible!*

"You hit your head ... memory got hurt. But you ... okay."

"How d-did I get here?"

"An ambulance brought you."

I yelled, "What's going on?"

"Mary. Be calm."

"WHERE AM I?"

"Honey. You're in the hospital. Everything's going to be okay."

A woman walked in and smiled. "I have something to help you feel better, dear." She touched a box beside the bed.

Slowly, my frustration lessened. *What's happening?*

Confusion and fear clashed inside me. Exhausted, I felt myself slipping away ...

I SLOWLY WOKE, and saw a man standing close.

"I'm hurting—"

"The nurse is bringing medicine," he said.

Everything looked fuzzy.

"W-why can't I see?"

"What do you mean?"

"Um, there's f-four of everything—"

"Try blinking."

I did. It didn't help.

"It's blurry—"

"I'll tell the doctor."

I tried to remember what he'd said, but it was gone.

"Where am I?"

"In the hospital."

"Huh?"

"You were in an accident."

"How l-long have I b-been here?"

"Ten days."

"Why d-do I hurt so bad?"

"Your left wrist is broken. Your neck has two broken bones, and there are compression fractures in your spine. But the worst injury was to your head. Your car rolled over and over in the crash, and you hit your head and injured your brain."

"What crash?"

"Your car accident. You were in an accident and hit your head."

"I don't know my name ..."

"You're Mary. I'm your husband, Tom."

Husband? What's he talking about?

"Um ... will mam—UGHH!" *Why can't I talk?*

"Will my mam—my memory come back?"

"The doctor isn't sure how much of your memory will come back. But it's okay. If it doesn't return, we'll make new memories."

"Why c-can't I remember?"

"It's okay. Just rest."

Anger flooded me. "B-but I don't remember anything!"

"You had an accident on the highway. Your car rolled over several times. You hit your head, and your memory was injured."

THAT'S NOT RIGHT! my mind screamed at me.

"But it's okay, Mary. You're going to be okay."

Wait—what did he say?

I struggled to quiet the chaos raging in my head.

He straightened my covers.

Lost and scared ... sleep pulled me under.

I LOVED MY wife with all my heart, and wanting to prepare for whatever lay ahead, I stepped out of her room and found Dr. Baxter.

"Why can't she wake up?" I asked him again. "And why doesn't she remember me?"

"Mr. Parker, a TBI is rated as mild, moderate, or severe, and Mary's was severe. And the area of her brain that handles memory was bruised and damaged."

I pushed him to tell me more.

"The brain is normally surrounded by fluid to protect it from injury," he said, "but in Mary's case, it slammed through that fluid and hit the inside of her skull—in several places. The CT scan revealed that blood vessels in her brain were broken, and blood has leaked in her brain. On both sides."

He paused. "What was she like before the accident?"

"She had a busy life and was very alert."

"Really?" He pressed his fingertips together, regarding me curiously.

"Yes. She raised our children, is involved at church, works as a dental assistant, and has lots of friends."

"She worked a job?" he asked.

"Yes. She's been in her current job twelve years. And she's very good at it. So good, other dentists try to hire her away from her boss. She's very smart."

"Then she wasn't acting slow and groggy before the accident?"

"No. Not at all."

Worried for Mary and frustrated by the doctor's inability to know what she'd been like before, I turned away and headed back to Mary's room.

God, please help us.

HURTING AND DIZZY, I lay still, wishing the room would stop spinning.

A man entered the room.

"What's g-going on?" I asked.

"You're in the hospital. You're going to be okay, darling."

"Um ... wha—what?"

"You were ... accident."

"I can't—um, remember ..."

He spoke again, but I couldn't follow it.

My heart pounded. *What's happening?*

"I don't re-remember anyone ..."

"Your name is Mary. I'm Tom. Everything is going to be all right."

I d-don't know those names ...

I looked around—nothing was familiar. Tears welled up.

He touched my arm. "Darling, I love you." He leaned over and kissed my cheek.

I stared at him, then looked away. *Why did that man kiss me?*

He took my hand.

I shut my eyes and darkness swallowed me.

11

Stuck in a Loop

Ten Days After

Mary was alive, and I was thankful—but her mind was stuck in an endless loop of confusion. The seizures had become less frequent, but she kept waking with no memory, drifting, and falling back asleep. Her awareness showed little improvement.

Scared for her, I sat beside her bed, waiting anxiously for what would happen next.

I recalled the Sunday before the accident. We pulled into the church parking lot early, as we always did, ready to teach our Sunday school class. Mary and I loved those five- and six-year-olds. She greeted each one with a big hug, making them feel special, and their excited smiles warmed our hearts.

After class, we attended the morning worship service, and Mary sang a solo, "The Day He Wore My Crown." We'd been members of the church for eight years, and she sang a solo every few weeks. Each one reminded me of the first time I'd met her.

I BLINKED AWAKE, my eyes struggling to focus.

Why can't I see right?

A man slumped in a chair nearby, eyes closed.

"Hey," I called out.

He jumped to his feet and leaned over the bedrail. "How do you feel, darling?"

Darling? "Tired."

"It's okay. Just rest."

"I can't mem—remember—"

"You hit your head."

"Is that why I don't remember?"

"Yes."

"Will my memory come b-back?"

He hesitated. "Sometimes the brain remembers, and sometimes it doesn't. But you will be okay. I'll help you."

I lay still—trying not to hurt, trying not to be afraid, trying not to cry.

"Do you know who I am?" he asked.

"No."

"I'm Tom. And you're Mary. We're married. You—"

"When will my memory come back?"

"We don't know," he said gently.

My mind whirled.

"You might remember some things, but not others. You need to give yourself time to heal."

My emotions were in frenzy. Panic loomed on the edge of every moment, pulling me toward it while it threatened to swallow me. I struggled to calm myself.

Closing my eyes, I vanished.

AS MARY SLEPT, my mind raced.

How could this happen to her? *God, I'll do anything you want. Just let her be okay. I'll give up my job, my friends, everything, just let her come back to me.*

My life had entered a strange existence—my wife was drastically injured, I was living in a state of shock day after day in the hospital, and the medical team was using me as a bridge between them and Mary.

I kept praying for God's help.

Gravely worried for Mary's mental state, I spoke with the doctors each chance I got, hanging on to every word they said, desperate to learn everything I could. One of them told me that her awareness had just been tested.

"What does the testing show?" I asked.

"She was asked to respond by blinking or moving her hands. Her responses were slow and inconsistent, and she had varying levels of performance. That's not uncommon with a TBI."

"What can be done to help her?"

"We've started a medication to increase her alertness. But Mr. Parker, it could take a long time for her to recover from the TBI. And her recovery might never be complete."

"I understand."

I spent each day trying to comfort Mary, and each night, I dozed lightly in the waiting room, waiting for morning so I could see her again.

WAKING, I SAW a familiar-looking man standing by my bed.

He smiled. "Good morning, darling. It's good to see you awake."

"What's going on?" I asked hesitantly.

"You had a car accident. You've been here eleven days."

"No, that's not right ..."

"You're going to be okay."

"I ... I can't re-remember—"

"It's all right," he said gently.

Everything looked hazy and I rubbed my eyes.

"You'll be seeing an eye doctor for your vision problem."

Does he know about my blurry vision?

"Mary, do you remember I'm your husband?"

I stared. "No."

"It's okay. I'm Tom. I love you. Give yourself time, and things will come back to you. I'm going to go find a nurse to come check on you."

Worn out, I closed my eyes and sank into sleep.

I KEPT ASKING the doctors why my wife couldn't remember or understand anything.

One said, "Remember, her TBI was severe. Her condition may or may not improve. There's hope, but only time will tell."

Mary's waking moments were incredibly difficult.

It seemed impossible that the chalkboard of her mind had been wiped clean, and seeing her in that condition was painful, hard to comprehend, and scary.

I desperately wanted her to get better, but all I could do was try to answer her questions and help her be calm. My presence seemed to comfort her slightly, but her state of mind caused me agony. I fought to hide it as I struggled to show her only calm, love, and support.

God please, please help my wife.

Mary repeated the same questions over and over—who, what, where, why.

I worked hard to keep my voice soft, reassuring, and patient as I answered.

She couldn't remember anything she was told.

I OPENED MY eyes and saw the familiar man sitting beside my bed—and two young men entering the room.

"Hi, Mom," they said.

I stared, struggling to recognize them. The word *Mom* meant nothing to me.

One of them said, "Mom, do you remember—"

His words blurred, slipping past me. I shook my head. "No."

When they said they loved me, I said, "Thanks for coming to see me." I couldn't say it back—I didn't know if I did.

They lingered a moment, hesitant, before leaving.

Everything felt all mixed up.

12

Reminiscing

Sunday Before the Accident

As I drove us home from church, Mary and I talked about how our lives had changed through the years.

We were forty-two and forty-six, and our relationship had settled into something solid and treasured. Our three boys had grown into men, out in the world carving their own paths. We had the house to ourselves and enjoyed the stillness—the quiet tempo of our life.

That afternoon, I mowed the lawn while Mary knelt by the mailbox planting yellow flowers around its base.

When I finished, I walked over to her. "Your flowers look great," I said with a smile. "Almost as pretty as you are."

She laughed softly. "Thanks. I'll water these, then I'll be done."

"Hey, how about I take you out to dinner?"

She looked up at me, eyes playful. "A date?" she teased, pretending to think it over. "Well, that depends ... will you come to the front door and pick me up?"

I chuckled. "Sure, baby."

She laughed again—that easy, musical laugh I never got tired of hearing.

For our date, Mary wore a light pink blouse, her perfume drifting around her like a soft whisper of romance.

I told her how pretty she looked.

She smiled coyly.

At Longhorn Steakhouse, we sat across from each other, her hand resting gently in mine. As she shared the highlights of her week, I watched her closely. She looked years younger than her age because she took good care of herself, and I was proud to be her husband.

"I really love my job," Mary said, picking up her glass of tea. "It's fun, even when it's crazy-busy."

"I'm glad. The medical field suits you. You've got that calm, caring nature that dental patients like. They're lucky to have you."

She smiled. "How was your week at Sprint?"

"Not bad. Mike likes how I handle things, and I'm hoping to get a promotion sooner rather than later."

"That sounds good," she said softly.

I nodded. "Yeah."

We kept chatting as we ate—work, a movie we wanted to catch, the boys. Nothing heavy. Just simple, comfortable conversation.

Home again, we sank into the wicker chairs on the back porch, the warm evening wrapping around us. The sky blazed with gold, purple, orange, and pink. Mary's hand slid into mine, and the moment felt magical.

She sighed and whispered, "This is beautiful."

"I love our life," I murmured.

Her lips curved into a smile. "Me too."

We lingered, listening to the evening sounds around the lake. I felt a quiet contentment.

The future looked bright.

13

Doctor's Advice

Twelve Days After

The familiar-looking man approached my bed, holding two books.

"Mary," he said gently, "let's look at these together. One is our family photo album. The other is the church directory."

I didn't know what he was talking about.

He set the first book in my lap, opened it, and pointed to a picture. "That's you."

His eyes searched mine.

I stared where he pointed. Nothing made any sense.

"Um ... uh ..." I wanted to speak, but words were missing from my mind.

He slowly turned the pages. "Does anything look familiar?"

I shook my head. "I don't ro-room—ERGHH!"

Frustration surged through me. *What am I trying to say?*

"I can't remember!"

He softly patted my hand. "It's okay. I'm going to help you, Mary. Things will come back to you."

"Who are those g-guys standing by you?"

"Our boys. Your sons. Do they look familiar?"

"No. What are their n-names?"

"Dylan and Cody."

"Oh." I wanted to remember them but didn't.

Will I ever remember?

Worn out, sleep pulled me under.

I WOKE TO blazing pain in my head. The familiar man was sitting nearby.

"Hi, darling," he said quietly. "How do you feel?"

"Tired."

"I know you must be."

He stood, then leaned over and hugged me gently. "I love you."

I didn't move.

"Can I get you anything?"

"No." My voice was barely audible. *Why does he seem so familiar?*

"There's some of your family in the waiting room. Would you like to see them?"

Family? What family? "I don't know."

"Do you remember that some of them already came to see you?"

"No."

"That's okay. I'll go get someone." He stepped out of the room.

Confusion spun through my mind.

I WENT TO the waiting room. Mary's mother, brothers, and sisters sat together, their faces tight with concern.

"Mary's awake," I said, "and wants to see some people, but she's confused and not very strong. So you'll need to stay calm when you see her. Only two people at a time can come in with me, and each person can only stay a few minutes."

After a quick discussion, the family decided Mary's two younger sisters would go first. I led them through the ICU to Mary's room and stopped outside it.

"Mary gets upset and overwhelmed easily," I said. "To keep things simple for her, I'll go in first and tell her who's coming."

THE FAMILIAR MAN walked into my room.

"Mary, your sisters, Ginny and Lorraine, are coming in to see you."

Two women approached. I didn't recognize them.

Why are they talking so loud?

They left soon, and I sighed heavily. "D-do I know them?" I asked the man.

"Yes. But you're not close to them. Don't worry about it. Do you want to see more family?"

"I guess."

He nodded and stepped out. A few minutes later, he returned with two more women. The older one stepped close.

"Hi Mary," she said. "I'm your mother."

I don't know her.

The second woman stepped forward. "Hi, Mary. I'm your sister Lisa." She leaned over and gave me a hug, then said she loved me.

Not recognizing her, I stayed silent. Then the women left.

The door opened again, and two men entered. The older one spoke first.

"Hello, Sis. I'm your big brother, Joe."

I hesitated. "Um ..." His eyes were dark brown, and he was a stranger.

"I drove in from Oklahoma to see you," he said. "I've been very concerned."

I couldn't understand what he said. "Huh."

"I love you, Mary. Anytime you need me, just pick up the phone and call—day or night."

I didn't respond.

"I'm your brother Luke," the other man said.

A slender man with brown hair.

The familiar man spoke quietly with the two men before they left. Then he asked if I wanted to see someone else.

I struggled to nod.

A few minutes later, he returned with an older woman.

"Mary, this is your sister Meghan."

She spoke for a moment, then left. *Was she really a sister?*

Overwhelmed, I closed my eyes. Then I was told one of my sons wanted to see me.

A young man approached. He smiled as he stepped closer.

"Hi, Mom. I'm your son, Leo. I came into town from Oklahoma, with Joe."

Another stranger. "Um ..."

I turned my head toward the familiar man, standing beside my bed. He smiled and nodded. I looked back at my visitor. I tried to smile.

"It's good to see you," he said. "But my time to visit is short."

"Oh?" I didn't understand. *Did I forget my son?*

He left the room.

Nothing made sense. Fear, frustration, and despair weighed me down.

"I don't know anyone," I whispered to the familiar man.

"I don't know some of them much," he said. "Just think about getting better. Everything will be okay."

Exhausted, I faded away.

DR. BAXTER STEPPED into Mary's room, saw she was sleeping, and motioned for me to join him in the hallway.

"Tom, there's something I need to tell you."

"What is it?" I asked, closing the door behind me.

"I need to caution you to be careful about reintroducing people to Mary." His voice was calm but firm. "It's crucial to take things slowly—for her sake. It's important for her to have visitors, but it's also important to prevent her from becoming more overwhelmed than she already is. I know people want to see her, but she needs time to adjust, so she doesn't become more confused."

"Okay. I'll be careful."

"Any questions you have, just let me know."

He offered a reassuring smile, gave my shoulder a light clap, and turned to walk away.

I stepped back into Mary's room and settled in the chair beside her bed. As I watched her sleep, Dr. Baxter's words echoed in my mind. I'd hoped the interaction with family would spark her memory. She was upset by not recognizing anyone, and exhausted when those visits ended. I couldn't ignore the toll the visits had taken. It would be a fine balancing act between encouraging visitors and making sure she didn't become more overwhelmed.

I reflected on our children. The thought of her sons, once deeply connected to her but now strangers in her eyes, was a quiet sorrow. I also had concern for Mary's mother, siblings, and other relatives, and I hoped that in time, she'd recognize them. I knew that in the future, it would be my job to share the painful news of Mary's TBI with our friends and acquaintances, and it was paramount to protect her from further confusion during those encounters.

Lord, please help me know when and how to reintroduce people to Mary.

I sat there for a long time, holding her hand and thinking.

A new question occurred: *How can I help her find her way back to me and others when she doesn't even know herself?*

14

The Police

Fourteen Days After

I needed to call my boss with an update, but Mary's condition was too unstable. Everything was chaotic. I couldn't give Mike any answers—I didn't know what to tell him. The idea of returning to work was foreign. I pushed the thought of that call aside. It would just have to wait.

I went to the nurses' station. "Do you have any reading material about TBI?"

A nurse with kind eyes handed me two sheets of paper. "Here you go."

Disappointed it was all they had, I returned to Mary's room, sat down, and started reading.

Two policemen in dark blue uniforms walked into the room. The older one, a large man with black hair and piercing blue eyes, introduced himself in a deep, measured voice.

"We're here to ask a few questions," he said. "Just routine procedure following an accident."

Routine. As if any of this could somehow be considered ordinary.

The younger officer opened a notepad and held a pen ready. "Mrs. Parker, we need to ask you some questions. What can you tell us about the accident?"

She blinked, her brows drawn in confusion. "I d-don't know ..."

"What happened?"

"I don't re-remember ..."

I told the officers about her memory loss, but they continued asking her questions. She stammered but couldn't answer. When they told her she'd been in a car accident, she just stared blankly at them, eyes wide, uncomprehending. No fear, no recognition—just the void of the injury.

The younger officer closed his notebook. They both gave Mary a quiet "thank you" and turned to leave. The older one sent me a sympathetic look before following his partner out the door.

As Mary fell back into sleep I whispered, "I'll do anything for you, darling."

I'd watched the confusion in her eyes as they questioned her and knew the visit had been hard on her. I wished there was something I could do to help her. Her face was pale except for the fading bruises, and I wondered what would happen next.

Blocking out my shock and grief, I tried to think of everything I needed to handle. Dr. Baxter had said she'd need an aggressive course of cognitive therapy. What would that be like?

With all my heart, I wished I could help her. But how could I, when I didn't even know where to begin? I wanted to turn to my wife—my partner, my best friend—to get her help. Would I ever be able to do that again?

I have to be strong. Mary needs me to. She needs me now more than ever. Will her memory return? How will I take care of her?

I walked to the waiting room and sat down by Mary's brother Joe.

"I'm worried," I said. "I don't know how this head injury is going to affect Mary, or change our life."

He looked uncomfortable. A moment later, he nodded. "If there's anything I can do to help, let me know."

A woman walked up with a smile. I recalled that she was Debbie, one of Mary's former coworkers.

"Hi, Tom," she said, her voice soft and warm. "Want to join me in the break room for a little snack?"

I hesitated, unsure, then nodded. "That sounds good, Debbie. Thanks."

The break room was empty and quiet, save for the low hum of vending machines. We grabbed coffee and cookies, then sat down across from each other at a small table.

Debbie cupped her drink between her hands, her fingers tracing the rim. Her eyes never leaving mine, she smiled and leaned forward.

"How're you doing, Tom?"

I told her Mary's brain injury was hard.

She nodded slowly.

I went on, explaining the doctors couldn't say how much recovery there might be, and as I spoke, she tilted her head and leaned closer.

"Tom," she murmured, "you should leave Mary and move on with your life."

I blinked. *"What?"*

"You should think about it," she said, her voice deliberate. "She's badly hurt—"

"I'm not doing that," I said, stunned.

Her eyes searched mine. "Well, it's an option" she said, her lips curving in a knowing smile, "you might want to consider, an—"

Abruptly, I stood up, the chair scraping across the floor with a grating noise as I shoved back from the table.

"Excuse me," I muttered, and without waiting for a response, I turned and walked away, heading back to Mary.

TWO WOMEN CAME into my room and started rolling my bed.

"Where are you taking me?" I cried out.

"You no longer need the ICU," one said. "You're being moved to a regular room."

I stared at her, not understanding.

When they stopped rolling the bed, I looked around and saw the familiar man.

"Hi, darling. This is your new room," he said.

"Can I get a shower?" I asked.

"I'll go find out," he said and left.

He returned with a nurse. "The doctor okayed your shower," the nurse said. "But someone needs to be in there with you, and you must stay seated in a wheelchair." She smiled at me. "I'm off work now, but I'll take you to a roll-in shower."

"Uh—" I looked at the familiar man.

"She's very kind, Mary," he said, "and wants to help you."

"Okay," I said.

The nurse rolled me into a shower. Warm water fell on me, and my aching body relaxed. *What a good feeling!* When I looked down, I was met with the sight of big black bruises all over me. When the shower ended, my limbs were heavy from exertion and I was exhausted, but I felt refreshed.

The nurse helped me into a new gown, then rolled me back to my room, where I looked around for Tom, and—*Tom! I remembered his name!*

I searched his face, trying to recall anything else about him, but my memory was blank.

"Thanks for helping me get a shower, Tom."

His eyes lit up, and he grinned. "Of course, darling. Of course."

TOM TOLD ME that he and the children were worried about me.

"How many children do I have?"

"Just the three boys."

"Tell me about them."

"There's Leo, Dylan, and Cody. Leo is the oldest. He's married. Dylan and Cody are on their own, not married. You've been helping Cody plan his wedding—but honey, give yourself time. Things will come back to you."

With no memory of what he just said, I lay still while he adjusted my covers and patted my arm, and I drifted into sleep.

A YOUNG WOMAN entered my room. "It's time for you to start physical therapy," she said, jerking back my covers and lifting my legs and arms.

Tom stood close, watching. "Are you pushing her too fast?"

"No," she said.

Every move she made me do hurt worse. *Why is she doing this?*

"Let's get you up," she said, and started pulling me toward the edge of the bed.

Intense pain ripped through my chest. I cried out and struggled to breathe as the room spun, consciousness slipping away.

Tom grabbed me, carefully laying me back down as he angrily scolded the therapist.

I tried to take a deep breath, but unbearable pain stopped me. "Something's ... wrong," I gasped. "Can't breathe—"

The therapist glared at me, then whirled around and stalked out of the room.

"I'll get you some help," Tom said quickly and dashed out.

Time slipped by. My eyes opened. Tom stood there with another person. I didn't know why. Their voices were only noise, meaningless. My chest ached. Confusion washed through me, wrongness pressing everywhere. The room spun. Lost, I succumbed to sleep.

THE NURSE SAID quietly, "Tom, I need to get a chest X-ray."

A technician rolled in a machine and positioned it above Mary. After he finished, he stepped back, then rolled the machine away without a word.

The nurse met my eyes briefly. "I'll be right back," she said.

A few minutes later, she returned with Dr. Baxter. His expression was solemn.

"Mary's sternum is fractured," he said, "and a lung is collapsed. I'll change her physical therapy to compensate for it."

I nodded. "Mary needs a different physical therapist."

"I agree," he replied.

The nurse gently woke Mary and handed her a small breathing device. She explained that it needed to be used daily and demonstrated how.

Mary blinked up at her, confusion clouding her eyes. The nurse repeated the instructions, her tone patient.

Each day, I found myself reminding Mary that she had a device she needed to use, and how it worked. Every time, she looked at it as if it were new to her.

AN OLDER WOMAN walked into the room, her steps confident. "Hi, Mary. I'm your new physical therapist."

She slid an arm around me, steady and sure, gently urging me to stand. As she supported me, I forced myself to do it. It felt like a victory.

Later, another woman entered, a notebook held to her chest. She sat beside my bed, offering a reassuring smile. "I'm your speech therapist. What's your name?"

My name? My mind was blank. I stared at her, unable to speak.

"How old are you?" she asked gently.

I reached into the dark fog in my mind, trying to pull the answer out, but there was nothing there. *Why not?* I remained silent.

"Where do you live?" Her tone still calm—but thinner now.

Fear surged through me, and I looked at the therapist helplessly, willing her to understand. But her smile faded. She closed her notebook with a soft sigh and stood.

"We'll try again later," she said, already halfway to the door.

And then she was gone.

I can't live this way—it's impossible!

A doctor entered the room. He looked at me with puzzled eyes, then checked the clipboard in his hands. When he spoke, he asked questions I couldn't understand.

Frustration swirled through me.

Time passed in a blur.

15

Limbo

Mary's seizures had finally stopped. It felt like she was inching toward recovery, but I was keenly aware that each day she just lay in bed, looking around, barely moving, a lost expression in her eyes.

When people spoke to her, she was visibly agitated and didn't reply much.

With her words slurred, she asked the same questions over and over, and my heart wept as I tried to remain strong.

Deeply worried and unsure how to help, I kept a watchful eye on her and everything the medical staff did.

A MAN IN a shirt and tie walked into Mary's room. "Hello. My name is Dr. Odell, and I'm a psychologist."

He turned to Mary. "What's your name?"

She looked at me, panic flashing in her eyes. "I-I don't know," she murmured.

He frowned, shaking his head. "You're blocking your memories from coming back because you're afraid."

Mary blinked. I saw the confusion in her eyes—she had no idea what he meant.

"You can remember who you are if you try hard enough," he said.

Her hands trembled.

"Remember these numbers," he continued, then told her three digits. Then he said, "Having a good memory is very important." And he asked, "What were those numbers I gave you?"

She stared blankly at him. "W-what numbers?"

"Mary, do you know why you're here?" he asked.

Her eyes flickered toward me again, then back to the doctor. Her hands lay loosely at her sides. She didn't answer.

He sighed. "I'll come back in a few days."

As he walked out, the room fell silent except for the steady beep of the monitor.

Once he was gone, Mary slowly turned toward me, her eyes searching mine. "I don't like him."

I put a hand on hers. "I'll take care of it," I said.

"What?" she asked, her voice weak.

"You don't have to see that doctor ever again," I said.

OUR PASTOR, PAUL, a stocky man wearing a suit, came to visit again. The moment he saw Mary lying there, staring blankly at him, his eyes widened.

"What can I do?" he asked softly.

"Please have the church pray for us," I said, my throat tight.

He nodded. "You're already on the prayer list." Hesitantly he added, "Once Mary's home, people want to start bringing food and visiting."

I shook my head gently. "We need to take things slow—for Mary. She needs time."

Paul bowed his head and prayed, the words quiet and earnest. Then he left, and Mary and I were alone in the stillness of the room.

THAT AFTERNOON, I stood in the waiting room speaking with Mary's brother Luke, in hushed tones. The room was large, crowded with people, and the mood felt heavy with quiet emotion.

"Is there anything I can do, Tom?" he asked.

"I don't know—" I started, but broke off when Mary's mom came over and stopped beside me.

"You're not giving me enough information about Mary," she said, her voice sharp, eyes fixed on mine.

Surprised, I replied, "I've told you everything the doctors have told me—"

"Well, I'm her mother, and I have a right to know more!"

"I understand," I said, keeping my voice steady, "and I'll tell you when there's anything new."

I stepped back, giving her space, aware that Mary's condition was hard on her too.

THE NEXT MORNING, Luke approached me. "Tom, Mom wants to apologize to you."

I glanced around at the other families in the waiting room, hearing their quiet murmurs. "I'm willing to talk with her, but in the hospital chapel."

"That'll work," he said, nodding.

Later that day, I stepped into the chapel. The air felt calm and hushed, and Mary's family was gathered near the podium, conversing quietly.

As I joined them, Mary's mother looked at me with a somber expression. "Tom, I'm sorry for the way I spoke yesterday. I hope you can forgive me."

"Thank you, and I will, but right now, all my thoughts are with Mary." I looked around at their faces, each lined with concern. "I can't think about anything else. I need to get back to her."

"Okay. Thank you," she said.

With a heavy heart, I turned and headed back to Mary.

I STOOD AT the edge of my wife's bed, watching her blink up at me. Her awareness fluctuated from moment to moment.

"How are you feeling?" I asked, keeping my voice calm.

She stared at me, her eyes vacant.

I told her about the new psychologist I'd found— someone who specialized in brain injury, someone I hoped could help her.

She didn't respond. Her face remained still, expressionless.

I tried again. "He teaches other doctors about it. He's highly regarded, so he stays very busy."

"Uh-huh," she murmured, her voice flat.

I took her hand and gently continued. "He's actually a neuropsychologist, not just a psychologist. We're lucky to have him. As soon as you get home from the hospital, I'll schedule us an appointment."

Her eyes remained empty, like she was somewhere far away. I knew she hadn't understood me. I swallowed, squeezing her hand lightly, wishing I could reach her. She shut her eyes and drifted away.

I WAS LIVING in a dreadful limbo, not knowing what would happen next. The weight of Mary's injury and the uncertainty of how it might change her and our life together pressed on me.

Each day, she was growing slightly more alert, but her memory remained almost nonexistent. I rarely left her side, determined that she receive the best care possible.

Doctors moved in and out of her room constantly, expressing concern for both her and me. But they still couldn't offer much of a prognosis about the TBI. One of them told me that the best recovery from a TBI usually occurred in the first few years after it happened.

Years? I couldn't wrap my mind around that length of time. We were living moment by moment, from one unknown to the next. I wanted to know what the next second, the next minute, the next day held for Mary.

CONFUSION WHIRLED INSIDE me. Trying to remember anything didn't work—my memory was blank. Everything happening around me was a jumble.

"Tom, what happened to me?"

"You were in a car accident."

"Why can't ... why can't I remember?"

He frowned. "I don't know, but it's okay. Just rest."

"But I want to remember! My memory is gone. Why?" I felt like crying and screaming.

"Maybe it'll get better, Mary. I hope it will, but don't worry about that for now."

"But why don't I remember?" Tears pooled in my eyes.

"Because your brain was shaken hard, and it hit the inside of your skull and got bruised. And that injured your memory."

I felt terrified. *Who am I? What kind of person am I? How can I live with no knowledge of myself?*

Tom started talking about other things, but I was in so much pain he left to go find a nurse.

I SAT BY Mary's bed, watching her fidget restlessly. Her TBI was so bad, what could her future possibly hold?

A knock on the door interrupted my thoughts. When I opened it, I found Mary's boss, Jim, and her coworker Ellen, standing in the hall.

"Hi, Tom. How's Mary doing?"

"Her car rolled over and over on the highway, and her brain injury is severe. Come in."

They stepped inside and Mary stared blankly at them. Shock flashed across their faces. They tried to talk to her, but she remained silent.

TWO STRANGERS HAD stepped into my room. *I don't know them.* A wave of guilt washed over me. *What am I supposed to say?*

I couldn't make sense of anything. My head never stopped spinning. Everything frustrated me.

Will I ever wake from this nightmare?

Tom spoke with the strangers, and they left.

I looked at him and felt comforted. I didn't know why. *What was our relationship?* I rubbed my forehead.

How can I live without my memory?

Tom said something to me, but I couldn't understand his words. I saw sadness in his eyes.

Something flickered in my mind, but just as quickly, it was gone. *Was that a memory? How am I supposed to know?*

Each moment was a painful grind—turmoil and frustration my constant companions.

I couldn't tell what was real and what wasn't.

Am I losing my mind?

Or is it already gone, and I just don't know?

Later, as I slept, a dream came alive.

The car rolling ... metal screaming ... a hallway ... bright light ... someone standing there ... my dad? who else? ... they said something I need to remember ... I'm reaching for the words ... but too far away ... they fade ...

I NEEDED MORE information about the TBI, so when Dr. Murphy, the neurologist, entered Mary's room again, I asked her to help me understand it better. I spoke quietly since Mary was sleeping.

Dr. Murphy walked me through it.

"Her brain has what's called a coup-contrecoup injury. That means it was damaged in multiple areas. Each area of the brain handles different functions. In Mary's brain, some of the areas were badly bruised, and she has amnesia."

"Will her memory heal?"

Dr. Murphy drew a slow breath and clasped her hands together. "I'm sorry, Tom. It's impossible to know."

Then, to my surprise, she said Mary would be discharged in a few days. She added that her recovery from the TBI would require rest, a slow return to activity, and that it could take a long time.

16

Family Dinner

As Mary continued sleeping, I sat beside her bed considering what Dr. Murphy had told me. *Would she ever remember me? Herself? Our boys?*

I closed my eyes, seeking a moment of calm, but instead, I was transported back—back to the Friday before the accident. It seemed like a lifetime ago.

When I arrived home after work, Mary came out of the kitchen, met me with a quick kiss, and asked, "How was work?"

"Fine."

After changing into a polo shirt and blue jeans, I joined her in the kitchen. The aroma of home-cooked food filled the air. She was a great cook—one of many things I loved about her. As she stirred a pot on the stove, I stood at the counter and mixed a salad.

"So, what did you do after work today?" I asked cheerfully. She usually arrived home an hour before I did.

"Laundry. You know how I love that," she smiled. "Will you hand me the salt, sweetheart?"

"Sure." I passed the salt after stealing a quick kiss, enjoying her perfume.

We discussed our day as we finished preparing dinner, laughing several times.

Dylan and Cody had only recently moved out of our house and tonight they were back for a family meal. They came into the kitchen with smiles on their faces, hungry and ready to lend a hand. Dylan filled glasses with iced tea, while Cody set the dining table with plates and silverware.

After dinner, we played spades. We all loved the game. The sound of shuffling cards and laughter created a sense of comfort. Of home. Then the boys headed back to the apartment they shared, and Mary and I snuggled on the couch and watched TV.

As I reflected on that evening, I wondered again if Mary's memory would ever return.

17

Fainting

Eighteen Days After

I finished a quick breakfast in the hospital cafeteria, then headed down the hallway toward Mary's room. Whenever someone tried to get her out of bed, she usually fainted, and I needed to talk with the doctor about it.

Just as I reached Mary's door, Dr. Li appeared—an internist. He didn't waste a second.

"Mr. Parker, Mary has vasovagal syncope."

"What's that?" I asked.

"Something is triggering her heart rate to suddenly slow down, making her blood pressure drop. That's why she keeps fainting. Did she faint a lot before the accident?"

"No, never. What can be done about it?"

"I've prescribed a medication. It'll keep her blood pressure up."

I prayed it would work.

MY HEAD HURT so bad I longed for sleep.

Confusion surged through my mind in a never-ending storm. As I lay trying to endure it, something whispered faintly at me. It was gone before I could reach for it.

I was living in fear and afraid someone would find out.

People kept coming and going in my room. I had no idea why. When anyone spoke to me, their words were mostly just noise I didn't understand. Whenever I tried to speak, people's faces usually looked confused.

The feeling that others expected more than I could do haunted me.

A nurse tried to get me out of bed, but the room started to whirl. I went limp and nearly passed out.

TOM WALKED INTO my room, his eyes finding mine the moment he stepped through the door.

"How are you feeling?" he asked.

"I can't stand how confused I am!"

He took my hand—his fingers warm and strong. "You're going to get better. Just give yourself time." He hugged me gently. "I love you. And I'll help you."

I leaned back and looked in his eyes. "When will, um, Leo come ... come see me again?"

I remembered his name!

"Honey, he had to go home. Back to Oklahoma."

A wave of sadness hit me.

"He didn't want to say goodbye?"

"He did. He and your siblings and your mom all came and spent time with you yesterday, before they left. They told you they had to leave and go back to Oklahoma. You don't remember?"

I searched my mind but couldn't pull up a single shred of what he described.

"No."

"They didn't want to leave, but they had to," he said.

I sat in silence. They were gone. They had lives to get back to, and I was stuck in the hospital.

18

An Unexpected Change

Nineteen Days After

A doctor stepped into my room and said, "Good morning, Mary. I've got good news. You're going home tomorrow."

What?

I blinked at him, trying to understand.

"You've been here nearly three weeks," he continued. "You're being discharged. It's time to start the next phase of your recovery."

His words slammed into me as I realized what he was saying. I sat up straighter, heart pounding.

"I ... I don't want to leave. I need to stay here."

He stood at the edge of my bed, nodding. "There's nothing more we can do for you in the hospital and it's time for you to go home."

My stomach dropped. I could barely breathe. Disbelief welled inside me. "You want me to *leave*?"

"I've spoken with all your doctors. We believe it's time for you to continue healing at home. Being in familiar surroundings may help your memory return."

It felt like the ground beneath me was disappearing. "But how will I see the—the doctors I see here?"

He smiled. "Your husband will take you to their offices."

And just like that, as quickly as he had appeared, the doctor was gone—taking with him the only security I had … my room.

As I lay on the bed, a swirl of emotions consumed me. I tried to figure out what was happening, tears streaming down my cheeks.

Home. They said I'm going home. A place I don't know …

Tom walked into the room, then rushed forward, sat on the bed, and took my hands in his.

"Darling, what is it? What's wrong?"

"I'm being sent home," I choked out. "But I don't remember it."

His expression changed and a broad smile spread across his face. "Really? Mary, this is great news. Why are you upset?"

I stared at him in disbelief. *How could he consider this great news?*

"Because I don't remember anything!" I cried out. "I don't know home, so how can I go there? It doesn't make sense! I don't understand. This is all I know. I need to stay here."

He wrapped his arms around me in a gentle hug. "It's okay. I'll be here with you. I'm going to help you remember home. We can do this."

I paused. His confidence was comforting.

"Oh?" My trembling voice was muffled against his shoulder.

"Darling, it's going to be all right. I promise."

Pulling away, I looked at him. "I don't know what to expect when I get there. I don't even know if I'll recognize it."

"It'll be an adventure then." He smiled. "You'll get to see our home for the first time, through new eyes. That's a gift, Mary. All of this—the fact you're here—it's a gift. And I'll help you, every day." He wiped my tears away with the back of his fingers.

I scanned his eager face, wishing I could see things the way he did, with his optimism.

"Nothing else is familiar, so how will I recognize home?"

He smiled, pulled me close again, and brushed his lips against my cheek. "You don't have to worry about that, honey," he said quietly. "If it's not familiar, you'll have new things to discover. I'll be with you. We can do this."

I sighed and closed my eyes.

Could I do it?

I WOKE TO the sound of rustling and saw Tom putting things into a bag.

"What are you doing?" I asked.

He smiled. "You're coming home today. Remember?"

"No." Fear crept through me. *Home?*

My tiny room was the only place I knew. The outside world was a mystery.

A nurse appeared, moved me into a wheelchair, and pushed me down a hallway toward something I couldn't even begin to imagine.

My stomach twisted into a knot. *This can't be happening—I don't want to leave.*

But it was happening, and there was no stopping it. The nurse wheeled me out the hospital door and I saw Tom standing beside a car, smiling. The anxiety cascading through me slowed, and I breathed a little easier.

He loaded my walker into the back, then carefully helped me into the front seat. He pulled the seatbelt across me, latched it, and kissed my cheek.

Everything felt surreal.

Starting the car, he said, "Darling, I'll turn the radio on for you. You love music."

I gripped the armrest tightly as he drove.

He turned onto a street with brick houses, sidewalks, and green manicured lawns. "This is our neighborhood," he said. Then he pulled into the driveway of a two-story house with white columns and a brick front porch.

"Is this home?" I asked.

"Yes. Does it look familiar?"

I searched my mind—nothing.

Too scared to speak, I shook my head.

He helped me out of the car and up the front steps to the porch. As I leaned on my walker, he unlocked the door and pushed it open.

"Take your time," he said, putting a hand lightly on my back.

I took a deep breath and pushed the walker into a foyer, searching for something that would tell me I'd been here before. Light tan walls, a gold-framed mirror, a table with a pile of mail—nothing rang a bell. I heard the click of the door closing behind me and suddenly felt safe. I glanced at Tom, searching his eyes, and he smiled at me.

Wanting to find something I'd remember, I went around a corner and saw a large living room with a cathedral ceiling. I studied the wall of windows, the bookshelves, the pictures of landscapes, a fireplace. Through the back windows, I saw a quiet lake.

Was this home really mine? I searched my mind, willing a memory to return—but nothing came.

"It's so good to have you home," Tom said.

With a sigh, I settled onto a leather couch, my emotions in turmoil. Tom sat down beside me. He didn't speak, letting me take everything in.

Removing my neck brace and the splint on my wrist, I tried to calm myself. I was lost. I remembered nothing of myself, and now, apparently, of my home.

How did I have a life that others remember, but I don't? God, help me.

Something streaked across my mind, startling me. I tried to grab it, but it was gone.

Was that a memory?

The safety and security I'd felt a moment before crumbled. Tears welled up. My hands shook. "Tom, I can't—"

"It's okay, darling." He pulled me close, his embrace warm and soothing. "It's going to take some time for things to come back to you. You just need to give yourself time. You can do this, and I'm here with you. I believe in you."

How can I do this? Can I start my life over?

That evening, I went through the motions of getting ready for bed in a room Tom said was ours. Nothing felt familiar. I kept trying to make sense of things. He pointed to the side of the bed I apparently slept on. The covers felt comforting as I slid beneath them, a sharp contrast to the confusion whirling in my mind. Who was I? And who was Tom?

When he slipped his arm around me, I didn't question it and fell asleep almost instantly.

AS MARY'S BREATHING settled into a steady rhythm, my thoughts began to drift. I had promised to stay beside her all night in case she needed anything.

The house was quiet in a way the hospital had never been. No monitors. No people moving in and out of the room. No one else responsible for her—just me, with the sound of her soft breathing and the weight of what it meant that she was home. Alive. Here. Mine—and also not.

I lay there, holding every memory of our life together, as the quiet of the night pressed in around me. A month earlier, my life had made sense. I'd known where I stood and who was standing beside me. Now, as I listened to Mary breathing in the dark, I wondered if she would ever know the man beside her.

The nightlight traced her face. She looked the same. Same cheekbones. Same mouth. I knew her by heart—how she liked the room cool at night, how she folded her socks into tight squares, how she liked her coffee. I knew the sound of her laugh before it started. But to her, I was only a presence. A voice in the darkness she lived in. A man who was a stranger.

I could look out for her, steady her, speak for her when she couldn't—what I couldn't do was give her back the life we had lived. In her mind, we had only just met. I couldn't return the mornings we spent laughing, or the evenings we sat close, saying very little because we didn't need to. I couldn't restore the double squeeze of her hand, when she wanted to say *I love you* without anyone hearing it. Those memories were mine alone now, like a language Mary could no longer speak.

In the dark, my instinct to protect her and provide for her strengthened—not through willpower, but through surrender. If this was the ground God had placed beneath us, then I would stand on it. If she was beginning again, I would be what didn't change—even if she never understood why, even if she never remembered she was my wife.

She moaned and shifted.

"You're okay. I've got you," I whispered.

As I stayed where I was, listening, the tears came. Quiet. Sliding down my cheeks.

I didn't know what the future held—but with God's grace, we would get through it.

19

Roller Coaster Emotions

Twenty Days After

I woke up and looked around—fear rising.

"Tom?" I cried out.

A moment later, he hurried through the door. "Let's get you up." His voice was low and warm.

He led me to a big kitchen. "Do you recognize anything?"

I shook my head.

"It's okay," he said. He handed me a glass of orange juice and some pills.

Frustration consumed me. Lost in the darkness of my mind, I was completely overwhelmed.

We stepped into another room, and I saw a piano. I ran my fingers across the top, stopping at a framed photograph of three boys.

"Tom?"

"Yes?"

"Um ..."

Something flickered deep in my mind. *A memory?*

I shook my head. "Nothing."

We moved into the living room. I felt like a visitor in someone else's house.

Longing for my memory, I sat down on the couch and struggled not to cry. I pushed myself as hard as I could to remember, but nothing came to me.

Desperate for help, I turned to Tom, my voice trembling as I whispered, "I don't think I can do this."

He took my hand and searched my eyes. "I know this is hard for you, darling. But keep trying. I know sometimes you're remembering little bits of things, and your thoughts are confusing, but it's okay. Things should get better in time."

He said I could get my life back together, but I didn't feel that way.

With almost no memory, my relationship with him remained a mystery. *Who is this man?*

A sensation of memory suddenly blinked in my mind, but it vanished just as quickly.

ONE UNSTEADY STEP at a time, I walked from room to room, trying to remember—trying to piece together a picture in my mind of the house. Walking was a precarious balancing act, clutching furniture and walls, my heart hammering with each shaky step. Everything was blurry, the room spun, the floor rippled like small waves beneath my feet. I often lost my balance and fell on my knees, frustrated and angry, fighting the urge to cry.

When I tried to think, my brain felt stuck, like it was trapped beneath a heavy weight, and I couldn't pull free.

I was living on an emotional roller coaster, constantly torn in all directions, hanging on for dear life—unable to see past the moment.

I was sure living was beyond me.

A BELL RANG, sharp and sudden.

"What's that?" I asked.

Tom smiled. "The doorbell."

Doorbell? "What?"

"Someone's at the front door," he said. "I'll be right back." And then he was gone.

Moments later, I heard voices and footsteps. Tom reappeared with a slender woman I'd never seen. She had golden-brown hair and seemed hesitant.

"Mary," Tom said. "Do you remember your friend Sherry?"

I looked curiously at her. "No."

"Well, this is your good friend from church, Sherry. You sang at her wedding."

She smiled, set down a container, and gave me a hug. But she was a stranger.

"It's so good to see you," she said. She picked up the container. "I brought lunch."

With no notion of what to say, I stared blankly and said nothing. After a moment of silence, she asked how I was doing.

"I—I don't know." I shrugged.

"Well, I think you're doing great," she said.

I felt awkward. We all sat at the breakfast table, and I struggled to eat and drink without spilling, unable to follow much of the conversation between Tom and the woman. Then she said she had to leave.

"Tom, I'll keep praying for you guys. If there's anything you need, please call me."

She hugged me again and whispered, "I love you, Mary."

As Tom walked her to the door, I sat back down on the couch with questions swirling through me.

Who is she? Is she really my friend? Maybe she's Tom's friend, not mine ...

Disjointed thoughts fluttered in my mind.

I heard the woman say, "I'll come back tomorrow."

Tom replied, "Thank you. I'll remind Mary what a good friend you are, later on, when she gets better."

Will I get better?

I heard him say goodbye to the woman. When he came back into the living room, I said sharply, "Why was she here?"

"Mary, she's your friend—"

"I don't know her! She's *your* friend."

His eyes widened, and he reached toward me.

"No, darling—"

"You like *her*, don't you? Not me." The memory of his smiling at her blinked in my mind, and sudden anger raced through me. My voice rose, accusing. "I saw you smiling at her and—"

"Mary, I love you. And you're the *only* person I love."

"You don't love me!"

"Yes I do!" He hurried toward me, his face filling with anxiety. "I love you *dearly*. Mary, you have a brain injury. From the car accident. And your memory got hurt. But Mary, I love you with all my heart."

He wanted me to believe him, but I didn't know *what* to believe. I didn't know anything.

"No! You don't!" I shook my head again, tears threatening to spill.

"Mary, no! Please. Listen to me—"

"I need you to get out of my house!" I struggled to stand, rejecting his assistance by waving him away.

"Oh, no, Mary—"

"I don't know you, and you need to leave."

I didn't remember what had triggered my need for him to leave.

"You've got to get out and leave me alone!"

Why does he look so sad?

"Mary. I love you!"

I looked at the stranger before me, his hands lifted from his sides toward me. *Who is he?*

"No. Go away!"

"Oh, Mary, don't do this—"

"GET OUT OF MY HOUSE! NOW!"

Surprise crossed his face. He dropped his arms and took a step back.

"Okay, honey. I'm going."

I watched him turn and walk out the front door, shutting it behind him. My heart pounding, I moved to the door and fumbled with the deadbolt before I heard it click into place. Feeling no better that he was gone, I made my way back to a chair and burst into tears. Alone with a mind I didn't trust.

DREADFULLY WORRIED, I stood on the front porch, thoughts racing. Rushing into the front yard, I peered through the living room window. She was sitting in her recliner, face buried in her hands, shoulders trembling as she sobbed.

I wanted to hold her and make her feel how much I loved her.

Hurrying back to the porch, I lightly knocked on the door. Waiting for the sound of the deadbolt to turn, I had half a mind to dash back to the window to make sure she was okay. But I forced myself to wait. And knocked again.

Then, at last, the sound of the deadbolt unlocking. I took a deep breath.

The door opened halfway, and Mary looked out, her face glistening with tears.

"Mary, I need to talk to you. Please. Can I come in?"

She hesitated, her lip trembling.

"I love you, Mary. You are the only woman in the world I will ever love. You mean everything to me. Always."

Another tear slid down her cheek. She wiped it away, sniffed, and looked at me with a bewildered expression. Her gaze lingered for a moment before darting away.

"I know this is a hard time for you, but please know that I love you. And I will do anything to help you. Anything. You can trust me, sweetheart. I promise."

She blinked, then dragged in a deep breath, nodded, and stepped back.

"Okay, you can come in."

Relief filled me and I stepped inside. "I love you. And I just want to take care of you."

"I'm sorry," she whispered. "I'm so confused ..."

Without another word, I reached for her. She came willingly, folding into me like a missing piece slipping back into place, and I gently wrapped my arms around her.

"I know, Mary. It's okay. We'll get through this together."

20

Lost in the Darkness

Three Weeks After

The darkness of memory loss wouldn't let go of me.

I struggled with how to do gigantic challenges—brushing my teeth, getting dressed, walking without falling—everything.

Tom was always there, supporting me, and each time I started to give up, he'd say, "We can do this." It was always "we," not "you." It created a feeling of hope inside me.

Four overlapping images of everything boggled my vision, but when I touched things, I knew my eyes were tricking me.

I was gripped by a sense of movement happening around me, sometimes slow and wavering, other times sudden and jolting.

Tom talked to me constantly and his voice stirred a feeling inside me, as though I'd known him before. I wondered what he knew about me. *Had we been close?*

New surprises lurked around every corner.

The doorbell rang. I managed to recall what it meant—a stranger was outside.

The idea of speaking to anyone felt impossible.

"Tom." I called out. "Someone's at the door."

When he opened it, a middle-aged man and woman stood there, holding a foil-covered dish. They spoke quietly with Tom for a moment, then left.

"Who was that?" I asked.

"The next-door neighbors," he said. "Our friends."

"I don't remember them."

Tom and I sat and talked, and a few faint whispers stirred in my mind.

"I've got an idea," he said. "Give me a few days, and I'll give you something that'll help you remember."

THROUGHOUT EACH DAY, I tried to spark Mary's memory.

"When you were a child living with your parents, what different places did you live?" I reminded her of good times we'd had with the children, like our recent trip to Six Flags amusement park. "Remember how much fun you had riding the roller coasters with the boys?"

Mostly she just looked away, but I refused to give up.

I wanted to whisper every memory back into her heart.

I pointed to photos in the family albums she'd made through the years and asked her what she remembered about them. I recorded her favorite TV shows, including *America's*

Got Talent, and talked her through them. I urged her to remember the children playing Little League baseball, and a family camping trip we'd taken.

Nothing seemed to trigger her memory.

MY DAYS WERE a haze of confusion and blazing headaches.

Life, the injury, the future—everything seemed impossible.

God, I really need your help.

I willed myself to pull memories from my mind, but nothing came.

Frustration kept building inside me, pressure rising until it snapped and my anger exploded.

When the storm struck, Tom's voice reached through the chaos, urging me to relax and think calmly.

He held my hands and prayed. "Lord, please give Mary the ability to do what she needs to do. Help us be patient and get through this. We trust you to help us. Amen."

Somehow, in those quiet moments of prayer, the fire inside me subsided.

I slept a lot, desperate to escape. I didn't know which was worse—the nightmare of my brain injury, or the nightmares in my sleep.

The nightmares woke me often, and gripped by fear my brain might never heal, I cried myself back to sleep.

MARY'S PROGRESS IN recovering from the TBI seemed negligible, but I kept believing it would happen.

Lord, please keep helping us.

I continued trying to give her good positive feelings and hoping they would stick—but for some reason it didn't work. Negative emotions constantly swamped her.

Yet gradually, I sometimes noticed the faintest flicker of recognition in her eyes. Fleeting, but unmistakably there.

PEOPLE TOM SAID were our friends from church started showing up, with smiles, food, and stories. I didn't recognize anyone.

When someone spoke to me, I struggled to understand what they said. Sometimes a voice triggered an odd sensation in my mind—like a ghost of memory brushing past.

When two people spoke at the same time, my head spun even faster.

One woman told me her name was Sherry. She said we were friends, and that the day after I left the hospital, she came by the house to see me.

But I had no memory of her.

Everyone kept looking at me as if they knew something I didn't—like they were waiting for someone to appear.

I had no idea who, or what, they were waiting for.

DEBBIE'S WORDS FROM the hospital echoed in my mind: *Tom, you should leave Mary and move on with your life.*

I ignored those words—I loved Mary and would never leave her.

I pushed myself to be the best caregiver and advocate possible, feeling my way through our strange new life, while clinging to hope for the future. As stress and sleepless nights wore me down, I wondered how my strength would hold out.

Mary's boss, Jim, had called me twice to check on her, expressing sorrow for her injury and her inability to return to work. "She was the best employee I've ever had," he said.

I was stretching my leave of absence from Sprint to the limit. Mike had called, saying he hoped I could return soon.

Slowly, Mary's speaking began to come a little bit easier, but the confusion clouding her mind remained nearly absolute. She remembered practically nothing about her life before—just a few disconnected pieces, like recognizing her piano but nothing else about it.

Around twice a week, she questioned me about some vague fragment of memory that had surfaced. Each time, my hope rose, but any fragments that came to her vanished quickly. Day by day, it was hard to tell if she was getting much better.

A shadow veiled her eyes, and her voice sounded hollow and distant. At times, when her thoughts seemed especially dark and dismal, I wondered if she'd given up on living. We were both overwhelmed, but I trusted God to help us.

I kept working to solve the puzzle of how to help Mary. Searching the internet, I found a Christian counselor we could meet with once a week.

MY DAYS BLURRED together.

I shuffled into the living room and sank into a chair, trying to pull a thought into my mind. When an idea began to appear, it slipped away before I could grasp it, like a whisper lost to the wind.

Desperate for even a single thought to stay with me, I pressed Tom with questions, hoping anything he said would stick. But nothing did.

The shambles of my mind was a tangle I couldn't unravel. Tears, hot and unstoppable, were my only means of coping. When the dam burst, I made no effort to wipe them away.

This is what hell must be like.

Random bits of vague thought floated in and out of mind, hard to hold onto. Even when I managed to keep one long enough to want to speak it, it usually disappeared before I could find the words. Sometimes my words came out, but in a twisted jumble. Other times, I could only blurt a noise. I desperately wanted to talk, but mostly, it was just too difficult.

I REMINDED MARY her neurologist was Dr. Murphy and took her to an appointment. I explained Mary's difficulty finding words and understanding what others said. Dr. Murphy asked question after question, most directed at Mary but answered by me. In the end, she ordered an MRI of Mary's brain.

When the results came back, Dr. Murphy explained that the scan showed the area of Mary's brain controlling language and speech had been affected by the accident. She told us that the struggle to communicate had a name, aphasia, and that for Mary, it was caused by the TBI.

I could see in Mary's eyes that she understood, even if only faintly, that Dr. Murphy's words were bad news. I wondered if she would ever be able to talk easily with others again.

Dr. Murphy said Mary should continue to improve as she kept working with her cognitive therapist and prescribed a medication to help Mary's concentration.

TOM STARTED TAKING me out to eat at fast-food places. He said it was a chance for me think about something other than the injury. We went to McDonald's or Chick-fil-A. Every excursion was scary, with difficult obstacles facing me—getting out of the car with my walker, navigating the restaurant, dealing with seating and what to eat, waiting while Tom went to order, trying to eat without spilling, and being around other people.

MARY WAS MARKEDLY different from before the TBI, and needing more answers, I took her to an audiologist who conducted an Auditory Brainstem Response test.

After the test the doctor said, "The results show abnormal activity occurring in Mary's auditory neural pathways."

"What does that mean?" I asked.

"Her hearing nerves must have been damaged in the accident."

ONE DAY I told Tom, "I remember something."

His eyes lit up. "That's great, Mary! What is it?"

"I know Jesus lives in my heart."

He smiled, wide and bright. "How do you remember that, but not other things?"

"I don't know," I said quietly.

He nodded, eyes softening. "Well, that's good. Keep remembering it. That'll help you."

AS I CONTEMPLATED how bad Mary's TBI was, memories of the life we had shared before surfaced in my mind.

Falling in love with Mary had changed my life. From the very beginning, there was a kind of magic that wrapped around us and wouldn't stop. She'd been confident, outgoing, and vivacious, with a laugh that was music to my ears and we loved laughing together.

Every weekend, I asked her out for dinner and dancing, and she always said yes. King's Table became our special place. The food and service were excellent, but the dance floor was the best part. It was in a separate room in front of a big stage, where a live band played rock music. We would dance together for hours at a time, and the rest of the world melted away.

Our relationship before the accident had been wonderful and precious, and now, I just had to keep finding ways to help her.

21

The Ring

Five Weeks After

"You need to get ready for a doctor's appointment," Tom said.

"I don't want to," I replied, tired of doctors.

"But you need to."

He handed me a different shirt to wear.

I frowned. "What's wrong with the one I'm wearing?"

"It has a coffee stain. You can't go out like that."

"I don't care," I said curtly, crossing my arms. "I want to wear it. It's comfortable."

He let out a sigh. "You need a clean shirt. You're going to a doctor's office, not lounging around the house."

"So what?"

"You need to look nice," he said gently.

I rolled my eyes but changed my shirt.

In the car, anxiety rose inside me.

"I'll drive slow," he said. "Try to help you be calm."

At the doctor's office, I sank into a chair. The doctor asked Tom questions, but exhausted, I couldn't keep up.

"TOM, HOW'S SHE been doing?" the doctor asked me.

"Her memory is barely functioning."

The doctor glanced at her. "Tell me how she's been acting."

"She's always confused. She knows she's having problems, and keeps asking why she can't remember."

The doctor turned to her. "Mary, how are you feeling?"

"I don't know," she mumbled.

"Do you remember me?" he continued.

"I'm not sure."

"I'm Dr. Davis, your psychiatrist. We've met before, and you can talk to me."

"I feel like I'm living in a nightmare."

The doctor asked more questions, but she didn't respond much.

ONE DAY, TOM told me he had something for me and handed me a little black velvet box.

"You said you don't remember the children very well."

"I did?"

He nodded. "You did. And what's inside will help you remember them."

I opened the box and saw a gold ring with five colored stones on the top. I stared, unable to take my eyes off it.

"How will this help me remember?"

"Those stones are the birthstones of you, me, and the kids. Now you can just look at your hand, and remember that we love you."

"Where'd you get this?"

"At the jewelry store. I had it made for you."

He smiled and slid the ring onto my finger, then lifted my hand and kissed it. "I love you, Mary."

My heart fluttered as a warmth went through me, and for a moment, the feeling of a memory stirred.

The ring was beautiful, and we talked about the boys and the relationships we all shared. A tangled mix of emotions whirled inside me, and tears threatened to fall. But tracing the contours of the ring, I felt a new trickle of hope. One thing was becoming clear: Tom's love was an anchor in my life.

"MARY," TOM SAID, "we need to go to the grocery store."

"What's that?" I had a vague idea but wasn't sure.

"It's where we get our food."

"Is it far?"

"No."

I was nervous about leaving home.

"Here's your walker," he said.

"I'm not going to use that anymore."

Alarm filled his face. "Why?"

"I don't like it."

"But Mary, you keep falling, and—"

"No!"

My heart pounded as Tom drove. *Shopping. Can I do it?*

When we pulled into a parking lot, I didn't recognize the place. Tom took my hand, and we walked across the lot and into the store.

The noise ... people moving around ... everything pressing in ... It felt like too much.

Unable to go further, I tugged on his hand. "Stop. I'm not sure—"

"Here, Mary, let's try this. Sit down here." He patted the seat of a motorized cart.

"I don't want to."

"You need to use this, darling. It'll make things easier."

I stared at it. *Too complicated.* How did he think I could drive that?

"I won't," I muttered.

"Mary, you need to ride this. You don't have your walker."

I glared at him.

Reluctantly, he pulled out a push basket. "Okay, hold on to this handle and walk with me."

I held on tightly as he guided the basket.

The store was scary—the sights and sounds all crashing together ...

A moment later, I couldn't handle it anymore.

There's too much! I felt like screaming.

"Tom, I can't do this."

Dizziness flooded me. *Oh God, please don't let me pass out.*

He patted my hand and kept moving forward. "You can do it. Keep holding on and push the basket. We'll start at this side of the store and go up and down all the aisles."

"I hate this place!"

I didn't know what I liked to eat and had no idea how to shop.

Why am I here?

"Just pick things off the shelf and put them in the basket," he said.

"What'd you say?"

He told me again.

I glanced around. So many items, all looking the same.

"How do I know what to get?" I asked.

"We need the basic things."

What does that mean?

I wanted to leave, but Tom walked forward. As he stopped to add something to the basket, I felt like I was aimlessly wandering around, in a place that made no sense.

Had I ever done this before? It seemed impossible.

Suddenly, I couldn't handle it another second. "I need to leave!"

"It'll only take a little longer. We're almost done."

"I hate it here! I don't ever want to come back. It's too hard."

"Mary, please just—"

"NO!" I shouted at him and grabbed his arm. "I want to leave! NOW!"

THE SHOPPING TRIP had been a disaster, but I'd managed to get most of what we needed. I hadn't meant to upset Mary, but I was living in a Catch-22 situation. She couldn't be left alone at home while I went anywhere, but grocery shopping was a huge challenge for her. She needed to be exposed to our normal routine to get her life back, but how in the world could she handle it?

Driving home, I reassured her, "Honey, we'll get better at this."

She sat still, her hands clenched on her lap. "I'm never going there again!"

"It's just going to take some time," I said soothingly. "I know it wasn't easy, but it's something we have to do. You'll see, it'll get easier."

Arriving home, Mary was spent. I handed her one plastic bag to carry. "Let's go inside," I said quietly, "and I'll put these away."

I followed her into the kitchen and watched in surprise as she placed her bag of groceries into the microwave oven and slammed the door shut.

She didn't know she'd done anything wrong.

"Don't worry about anything, Mary. Everything's going to be okay."

SIX WEEKS HAD passed since the accident and I'd missed work the entire time. I needed to return soon or lose my job, but Mary couldn't be left alone.

I called Cody and asked if his fiancée, Beth, might want to be hired to stay with Mary while I returned to work. She needed a job, but she was only twenty years old and inexperienced. Yet Mary had liked her before the accident, and she would soon be part of the family.

Thankfully, she wanted the job and agreed to start the following week.

Sprint agreed to relocate me to an office closer to home, with an earlier start time of 7:00 a.m. and a shorter lunch break. It was a good solution—I'd have more time with Mary each afternoon.

The next Monday, I put the new plan into action.

I'd explained the plan to Mary several times, but she couldn't understand it. She didn't remember Beth, or even care about an unknown woman being in her home, and my leaving the house each day was just another occurrence she had no thought about.

As I tried to settle into work, my thoughts were always on Mary. I called her several times each day to check on her, but she couldn't talk much, so I questioned Beth to stay informed. Every afternoon, I rushed home to be with her, and each night, I told her how much I loved her and kissed her goodnight.

ON FRIDAY, MY fifth day back at work, I sat in my office unable to stop thinking about Mary. She seemed okay with my leaving home, but even if she wasn't, she couldn't express it. With her weak cognition, she lived only in the moment—and I was missing those moments.

Then I made a decision. The accident lawsuit had concluded, and with the settlement from that and with our retirement accounts, we could make things work financially. I got up and walked down the hall and into my boss's office.

"I appreciate Sprint moving me to this location," I told him, "and I love my job, but Mary is hurt too much. I need to be at home to take care of her, so I have to quit."

The boss drummed his fingers on the desk and sighed. "I thought this might happen. We'll be sorry to see you go." He stood up and shook my hand. "But you need to do what's best for you and Mary." A resigned smile crossed his face. "I'll take care of the paperwork and mail your final paycheck."

We spoke for another few minutes, then I returned to my office and packed up my things, and with a sense of relief, I headed home.

When I walked into the living room, Mary was sitting on the couch, lost in TV. I sat down beside her, took her hand in mine, and looked into her eyes.

"Mary, I'll do anything for you. And today, I quit my job so I can take care of you full-time."

"Okay."

I'd become accustomed to her one-word responses and knew she was doing her best to process what I'd said.

"You are more important to me than anything in the world," I said softly, "and I want to help you get better. I'll do whatever it takes to make sure you have everything you need."

"I don't know what to say," she replied.

I knew she didn't understand what I'd done, but this was exactly where I belonged.

"You don't have to say anything, darling." I drew her close, holding her tight. "Just let me love you."

MARY STILL DIDN'T remember herself, me, or the children, except for a few fragments. The years of memories we had all once shared were mostly gone.

I'd lost the woman I'd known before, the partner whose presence and participation had made my world complete. And in her absence, I'd become a full-time caregiver. Mary needed help each day with even the smallest activities—it was like I was caring for a small child.

I carried the weight of our household alone, slammed— cooking, cleaning, doing laundry, paying bills, everything. Yet through it all, I loved Mary dearly and cherished every moment possible, hoping she could feel my love.

My biggest challenge, beyond dealing with the TBI and Mary's care, was not having enough time. We'd loved cooking together before the accident, so I had enough ability to prepare our meals. And since I'd always managed our family finances, that wasn't an issue either. I began sleeping less to have more time.

After tucking Mary into bed, I'd stay up late, and set the alarm for earlier. It helped me get things done, but I was tired and spread thin.

New hurdles popped up every day. Trying to handle everything was exhausting. Moments of uncertainty came to me unexpectedly, and I kept putting everything into God's hands.

I took Mary to endless medical appointments, sometimes two or three a day, determined that she get all the help possible. Our lives revolved around her appointments.

I continued taking her out to eat at fast-food places. It made feeding us easier, but even more, it presented her with different situations that nudged her to think as they came her way. Little by little, she faced the challenges, and I felt a quiet pride in her progress.

During one of these trips, as she stared at a menu, I realized she'd forgotten how to read. I added to my mental to-do list to try to help her relearn how.

Every day or two, friends would stop by with a meal or to visit briefly. A neighbor began cutting our grass each week. Some people offered to drive Mary to her appointments, but I turned them down. I needed to be there with her—listening, asking questions, protecting her, and making sure she got the best care possible.

I couldn't share my burdens with Mary. She grappled daily with the challenges of the TBI and couldn't do anything else. Although her memory remained practically non-existent, I kept encouraging her to believe she could remember. The responsibility for all our decisions was on me, and I worked hard to make only good ones.

Her fainting continued, whether sitting, standing, or walking. I brought it up at every medical appointment, but nobody knew how to stop it. The possibility of her falling and hitting her head again demanded extra vigilance—I couldn't let it happen.

I found a TBI support group for us and told Mary we'd start attending, but she couldn't understand the idea.

We were living moment to moment, and I was doing the best I could to hold things together.

22

Gripped by Hallucinations

Two Months After

Tiny pieces of thought whispered in my mind—vanishing before I could catch them. Were they memories? New thoughts? My imagination making stuff up?

I wandered the house in a daze, searching for a past I didn't recall. I lingered in the bedrooms Tom said had been the children's, wanting to trigger a memory, but nothing there meant anything to me. How could I have raised children and not remember? Was my mind hiding the past?

Desperate for answers, I pushed myself to remember—anything at all—but nothing came to me.

Without memories, it felt like the core of my being was missing. The thought my memory might never return was frightening.

Tom took me to lots of medical appointments, where I kept asking, "Will my memory ever come back?"

The response was always the same—there wasn't any way to know. Maybe it would. Maybe it wouldn't. And nobody seemed to understand the magnitude of my loss.

The absence of memories caused a feeling of emptiness. I didn't know how much longer I could handle it.

God, please give me back my memory. I don't know how to live like this.

Besides memory loss, other problems engulfed me. I always felt unsteady on my feet, like the world was rocking, and I couldn't stop falling down. When Tom drove us places, the billboards and road signs didn't stay still—they moved up and down in the air. Flashes of light flickered at the edges of my vision. Odd noises tugged at me, sounds that faded when I tried to listen. I heard voices talking and a baby crying. The baby's cry echoed in my head, and I searched the house over and over trying to find it, to no avail.

MARY HAD STARTED to recall the tiniest bits of our life before, but they came back jumbled and often worsened her confusion. I was grateful for even the smallest progress, but I missed the wife I'd known. I missed her singing, her laughter, her loving touch. I missed the woman she had been. And I continued to hope that God would bring her back to me. Day by day, I prayed for the strength to keep going.

I WALKED INTO our bedroom—and froze.

Four huge black dogs, overlapping each other, lay on the bed, staring straight at me.

Where'd they come from?

My heart racing, my hand shot out and gripped the doorframe.

They didn't move—just watched me with dark, unblinking eyes.

Unable to breathe, I forced myself to take a step back. Their eyes remained locked on mine.

Another step. Then I turned and ran.

"Tom!" I cried out, fear crashing through me.

He jumped up. "What's wrong?"

We sank onto the couch holding each other, and I glanced over my shoulder looking for the dogs. They were nowhere in sight.

"Nothing," I said, my voice shaking. "I'm tired. Hold me."

He wrapped his arms around me, pulling me close. Safe. Warm. My tears came slow and quiet.

LATER THAT DAY, the dogs returned.

I stepped into the living room and there they stood—staring, like they were waiting for me.

My throat closed in fear. Something was wrong. Terribly wrong.

"TOM!" I shouted.

He rushed in, alarm on his face. "What is it?"

"There's ... there's a dog—four dogs! Right there—don't you *see them*?" I pointed.

He blinked. "What are you talking about?"

I looked at Tom. "Those dogs—"

"We don't have any dogs, Mary." He looked baffled.

I looked back, and the dogs were gone. It was just Tom and me. "Oh—"

"Tell me what's happening," he said.

"I'll look around and suddenly see a huge black dog. The dogs. And he stares at me—all four of them!" I heaved a sigh.

"What?"

"They watch me."

"When does this happen?"

"I don't know!" I cried out. "I turn a corner, and they're here."

Upset, I wiped a tear off my cheek.

"Darling," he said slowly, "there's no dog in the house."

"Why do I see them?" I insisted.

He looked into my eyes. "I don't know, honey. But it's just your imagination. It's not really happening."

But it seemed so real, how could it not be? Fear swirled inside me.

Shaking my head, I started sobbing. "This doesn't make sense!"

He took my hands. I looked down at our hands together and drew comfort from his support.

"You're having hallucinations," he said, "and seeing things that aren't there."

My mind throbbed with the idea I was seeing things that weren't real, while I couldn't remember things that were.

"But it's real to me! Can't you understand?" I pleaded.

"Well, it can't hurt you." He pulled me close and hugged me. "Do you feel this? Do you feel how much I love you?"

I nodded against his chest.

"This is real, Mary. Think about this feeling, okay?"

"I'll try, Tom."

But I felt like I was going crazy.

He patted my back. "You need to give yourself more time to heal."

THE DOGS KEPT appearing.

Each time I saw them, I tried to remember what Tom had said, but my floundering memory barely worked. I complained to him again about the dogs, the baby, and other things.

He hugged me and prayed. "Lord, please help us. We ask you to make the hallucinations go away. Please help Mary heal. Thank you, Lord. Amen."

The words calmed me, and I felt a glimmer of hope.

AS I WATCHED MARY day after day, I became aware her cognition was worsening and I rushed her to the emergency room.

The admissions clerk barely glanced up as I explained the problem, not understanding my urgent pleas for help.

"You have to wait," he said flatly. "There's lots of people ahead of her, and some have more serious needs."

"You don't understand—"

"She'll wait her turn," he interrupted.

I glanced around the waiting room at the other people. But while I felt for them, Mary couldn't wait. I pushed the clerk again to admit her right away.

He refused again.

I guided Mary to a chair, worry pressing down on me with every step. She was fading, becoming increasingly listless and detached. An hour dragged by.

Then she passed out.

"Mary!" I cried out, trying to rouse her. She didn't respond. I shook her, desperate.

Seized by fear, I propped her up in the chair and rushed to the admissions clerk.

"She's unconscious!" I yelled at him, pointing frantically. "She needs help now!"

The clerk finally acted. He rushed a wheelchair over to Mary and she was wheeled to a room.

A nurse appeared, moving slowly, causing urgency to rise inside me again. She drew Mary's blood and unhurriedly left the room.

Minutes later, she burst back into the room, her movements frantic as she connected an IV line to Mary's arm.

My heart pounded as panic filled me. "What's happening?"

The nurse quickly adjusted the IV tubing. "Her potassium level is extremely low," she said.

"What does that mean?"

"If it gets too low, it can be fatal." Her voice was grim.

My stomach dropped. "How bad is it?"

"Dangerously low."

I pushed aside my anger at the admissions clerk who had delayed Mary's care, as I watched the slow drip, drip, drip of the IV fluid.

"How long until she's safe?" I asked, my stomach knotted with fear.

"We'll give her this bag of fluids, then test her blood again."

Mary was admitted to the hospital and closely monitored.

The next morning, she awoke delirious and hysterical with hallucinations. She wailed and thrashed about, eyes wide with fear. Frantically, she brushed her body to wipe off the bugs she insisted were crawling all over her.

"*AGGHH!*" She shrieked, waving her arms wildly at the ceiling and walls. "They're dropping on me!" she yelled.

I watched in disbelief as nurses tied her hands to the bedrails with strips of white gauze to keep her safe.

Seeing Mary in that condition, my heart broke for her all over again.

Standing beside her bed, I discussed the situation with her doctor. He was young and looked barely out of medical school.

When I told him Mary frequently hallucinated, he shook his head and frowned like he didn't believe it.

Knowing he was inexperienced, I tried again to make him understand, but the conversation went poorly.

"Mary needs a different doctor," I said, my voice unwavering.

His eyes narrowed, and he shook his head again and adamantly disagreed.

Without another word, I turned and strode out of the room, straight to the hospital administrator's office. I insisted to the secretary she let me see the administrator immediately.

Flustered, she quickly escorted me into his office, where I demanded that a different doctor take over my wife's care.

"That can't happen," the administrator said firmly.

A stern-looking man, in a white button-down shirt with a red tie, he sat ramrod straight in his chair, his gaze locked on me.

My determination increased. "Then I'm going to call an ambulance and have her taken out of here! Right now! Because I will not allow *that* doctor"—I pointed in the direction of Mary's room—"to be her doctor!"

I stood motionless, my eyes glued on the administrator, waiting for his response. The air was thick with tension.

He stared at me for a long moment. Then, he took a deep breath and finally spoke. "Okay. I'll change her doctor."

It was another step of progress in the relentless battle for my wife's health.

Shortly after I returned to Mary's room, the new doctor arrived—a sharp-eyed, older, more experienced man. I filled him in on everything, from Mary's accident and TBI to the fainting and hallucinations. He listened attentively, and we talked about her care. In that moment, I knew she was in better hands.

Over the next two days, the hallucinations faded away. The doctor prescribed a medication to keep them away, and I took my sweetheart home.

23

The Mary I Knew

From the first day we met, it was clear to me there was a magical spark between us. With each date we had, the attraction between us grew until we didn't want to be apart.

Mary fit easily into my life. She loved that I adored her, and she made me feel cherished. Her joy, her lightness, her laughter—she made life fun. In response to my attempts to be romantic with her, she sometimes responded in a playful, dramatic way that was amusing and entertaining, and made us laugh. Her laughter was beautiful.

It became a running joke between us that Mary was a hopeless romantic, while I had no romantic bone in my body, and I simply made allowance for her loving nature. But truthfully, I found her charm irresistible. There was something about her that drew romance out of me, and I wanted to give her everything I could.

She held a special place in my heart, but we had different views on how to raise the children. She would let them slack off a little more than I wanted, like letting them leave their clothes, books, and other items lying around the house too much. With my military background, I liked a house that was neat and organized.

One evening, I came home from work and walked into the living room and found Cody's shoes, red and white high-top sneakers, once again strewn in the middle of the floor. Since Mary and I had given him numerous reminders to stop leaving his shoes lying around, I picked them up and crossed the living room to the glass door at the back. Not hesitating, I launched the shoes into the backyard, the thuds of their hitting the ground echoing in the quiet evening air.

Mary's eyes went wide with surprise. "Why'd you do that?"

"Maybe now he'll stop leaving them lying around the house," I said with a chuckle.

She smiled at me, a mischievous glint in her eyes, a soft laugh bubbling through her lips. Both of us were curious to see how Cody would react when he came looking for his shoes.

When he entered the kitchen, Mary and I waited for the inevitable questions about his missing shoes, which, of course, followed soon after.

We told him what had happened, and reminded him he'd been repeatedly told not to leave his shoes lying around.

"Wait," he said, his face filled with astonishment. "You actually threw them outside?"

I nodded. "And if I find them lying around again, it'll happen again. You need to be careful to not leave things where they don't belong."

He opened and closed his mouth in disbelief, speechless, before heading to the back door. I hadn't bothered to tell him that from my spot by the window, I could see where his shoes had landed.

Mary stifled a laugh, and when we heard the sliding door open and shut as Cody went in search of the shoes, she threw a dish towel at me playfully and allowed her laughter to escape.

"I can't believe you did that," she said. "But I bet he won't be doing that again."

Those were the kind of things I wished Mary remembered. We had both loved our little dance of life together. She took care of me, and I took care of her, and together, we created a loving marriage, and a stable, happy, and nurturing home for our family.

I missed "my" Mary, but maybe in getting to know this new one and telling her stories about our life together, I could find her again.

24

One Step at a Time

Three Months After

It felt like my life had been erased, as though I hadn't existed before.

Now and then, a fragment of thought flared, streaking across my mind and vanishing before I knew what it was, leaving me grasping at emptiness.

In the darkness of my injury, Tom remained a stranger. When he said we had been in love, I wished I could remember what that felt like. *What did I lose?*

He took me to our first appointment with Cathy, a counselor with snow-white hair and a soothing voice. I perched on the edge of the chair, gripping my knees, struggling to explain how bits of thought flickered and faded, never lingering long enough to seem real.

"Mary," she said, "there's always hope, no matter what you're facing, that things will get better."

THAT AFTERNOON, AS I pushed myself to remember the meeting with Cathy, suddenly—

BANG ... crashing ... rolling ... slam ... walking toward a light ...

My hands shaking, I took a deep breath and reached for more.

But my brain refused to give me anything else.

It only gave me what it wanted to, and it was never enough.

I tried to hold on to the memories, but they were already slipping away.

Tom walked into the room and asked, "You okay?"

I nodded through the tears sliding down my face.

"I remembered something," I whispered. "It came fast ... then it was gone."

He sat beside me. "That's still something," he said gently.

"I want my memory to come back."

He nodded. "Just give yourself time."

EVERY DAY, MARY kept asking me questions. Often the same ones. Or slight variations. Her eyes searched mine, her hands fidgeting in her lap. She was always probing. Always looking for clues to who she was. For meaning.

I wrestled with how to answer, hoping my words would spark her memory and trigger new thoughts.

As she struggled with even simple little tasks, I kept encouraging her. But often, she still didn't understand what was said. And when she did, her inability to retain it for more than a moment left her continuing to flounder.

Watching her struggle was heartrending.

She'd stare at the coffee maker, then snap at me because she couldn't remember how it worked—no matter how many times I explained it.

I weathered those outbursts as best I could, knowing my difficulties were nothing compared to hers.

I KEPT HOPING my memory would give me more. With my past mostly hidden, I felt like a stranger to myself.

Who am I?

When I looked in the mirror, I didn't recognize the woman who stared back.

Everything felt too hard.

"Tom, living with the injury feels like climbing a mountain that never ends."

"You just need to give yourself more time to heal," he said gently.

I was living minute to minute and couldn't fathom anything beyond that. *What does more time mean?*

I tried to pray, not knowing if my words made any sense.

ONE DAY, TOM took to see my personal physician, Dr. Anderson.

I didn't remember him—a thin man in a shirt and tie, a stethoscope draped around his neck, sleeves rolled up to his elbows.

I described my feelings, and he prescribed something new—anti-anxiety medication.

As we walked out of the office, Tom said, "I love you, Mary, and it's okay you feel this way. We can get through this."

Something in his voice stirred a faint memory, like a whisper in the fog, calming me.

"I don't know what I'd do without you, Tom."

He gently urged me to believe in myself and that things would improve.

MARY'S MEMORY FLUCTUATED constantly, between practically gone and barely there. Her mind kept inventing ideas that she believed were real memories, which caused more confusion and stress.

Her insistent questioning sometimes waned, but it always returned. Answering her questions had become a full-time job, demanding more patience than I ever thought possible. I knew it was important to give her every answer I could, and the responsibility of keeping every detail accurate pressed heavily on me.

I tried teaching her to accomplish a task by taking one small step at a time.

"When you need to do a little task or climb a mountain," I said, "don't look at the end of the task or the size of the mountain. Look at the first step, and after you complete that, look at the next step. Doing things one step at a time is how to get things done."

TOM TOOK ME to a brain injury support group meeting. I walked in unsure what to expect. What I found surprised me—people who had a brain injury, who welcomed us and were happy. Some even laughed about their problems in lighthearted conversation.

About twenty people of various ages were there, and everyone was friendly. Realizing that others were living through the same nightmare I was brought a strange comfort—I wasn't alone.

I relaxed and began to enjoy the camaraderie.

Then the group leader asked everyone to pull their chairs into a circle and started the group conversation with, "Brain injury is an invisible injury."

That hadn't occurred to me, but I realized it was true. *People can't see my injury—it's invisible to them.*

Group members took turns talking, and some of their situations were very different from mine. Hearing the stories of other survivors sparked something inside me, and for the first time, I started to think that maybe I wasn't going crazy.

I learned I was called a "survivor" and Tom was a "caregiver." In that moment, I saw myself in a whole new way: *I'm not broken—I'm a survivor!*

One member said his brain injury made him feel like his brain was running the bakery while he was just tasting the cookies. Everyone laughed.

After the meeting, Tom and I agreed it had been more than comforting—it had also been very informative.

TOM ARRANGED FOR me to have a private counseling session with Cathy, just the two of us, while he waited in the lobby. She asked me lots of questions, including how Tom and I were getting along.

"We're fine," I said. "I'm learning things about him. There's something in the way he looks at me that makes me feel a little better."

I paused, wondering why I'd said that. It didn't make sense—it was just a feeling that puzzled me. I tried to focus on the rest of the session, but my thoughts kept drifting to Tom.

As he drove us home, I thought about how much I enjoyed his company, then the thought faded in my mental fog.

WE WENT TO our second support group meeting. One member announced to everyone, "My injury happened twenty years ago, and I'm still working to recover."

I leaned toward Tom and whispered, "That will not be me."

"You never know what the future holds," he whispered back.

When it was my turn to talk, I took a deep breath and began to speak about my accident, then—

BANG! The steering wheel clenched in my hands, screeching tires, spinning, rolling, slam—

Abruptly, the memories stopped.

My heart pounded. The vivid memories had seemed so real, it was like I'd been right back in the accident. The room swirled around me. Everyone stared as I sat frozen, unmoving.

"Are you okay?" Tom asked.

I slowly nodded. Someone asked me to tell them more, but I couldn't speak.

Tom smiled and took my hand. I twined my fingers tightly into his, comforted by his support, and tried to pull myself together.

What's happening in my brain?

The answer didn't come.

But the next week, we attended again.

And we became regulars.

"DARLING, WOULD YOU like me to take you to have your hair cut and colored?" Tom asked.

I had no clue about my hair. "I don't know."

"That's okay," he said gently. "You've been seeing your stylist a long time and she knows how you like it."

The thought of getting a haircut, or liking a certain color, felt strange.

"What if I don't like it after it's done?"

"It's just hair, and it'll grow back," he said, smiling.

Suddenly upset, I said loudly, "Why don't you like my hair?"

"I do like it, but I thought you might want to have it cut."

"My hair is fine!"

He took a deep breath. "I think you need a cut," he said softly, his eyes meeting mine with sincerity. "And I think you'll enjoy getting it done."

As with almost everything, the whole idea felt odd. But I agreed to give it a try.

At the salon, he introduced me to a pretty redhead with a little rose tattoo on the inside of her wrist. She said she knew me.

I didn't recognize her.

What does she know about me?

While she worked, she mentioned that Tom had told her about my head injury. I didn't know what to say and stayed silent.

"Okay, Tom, I'm done," I said when she finished.

He looked up from the couch where he was reading a magazine, surprise crossing his face.

"Darling, why'd you choose that color for the highlights?"

"I don't know," I said.

"Well, you've never done purple before, and I think your previous color looked prettier. Would you let the stylist change the highlights back to a lighter blonde for me?"

I hesitated, wondering why he didn't like purple, then nodded. The stylist redid the highlights, and when she was done, Tom grinned at me.

"You look beautiful," he said. "Do you like it?"

"Yes," I said softly, my lips barely parting as I thought about his compliment.

He asked if I wanted to get my nails done, and once again I hesitated, not knowing what I wanted. He suggested a pink color, so I let another woman do my nails.

On the drive home, I flipped down the sun visor and peeked in the small mirror, examining my hair. Sunlight streamed through the windshield, making it shine. I patted it, then let my gaze drift to my freshly painted nails, marveling at the soft pink.

Tom gave me an admiring look, and I felt my cheeks flush.

"You know," he said with a chuckle, "you look really pretty."

"Thank you," I murmured, letting out a small laugh as I wiggled my fingers.

"Mary," he said quietly, "you should get your hair and nails done whenever you want. Okay, darling?"

There was no pressure in his voice, only gentle encouragement. It settled over me, strangely comforting.

"Okay."

I glanced at him as he drove, and my heart skipped—a little flutter that surprised me.

"Thanks, Tom."

He reached over and patted my hand briefly. The feeling of his touch lingered longer than I expected.

"Hey," he said, "you deserve to be happy."

I leaned back, smiling out the window as the trees passed by, a thrill humming quietly through me.

25

Overdosed

Tom suggested we try returning to church. I agreed, wanting to believe I could handle it.

Sunday arrived too quickly. As I got dressed that morning, my hands trembled with apprehension. By the time we pulled into the parking lot, my heart was racing.

Tom reached for my hand as we walked inside. I held on tightly to keep myself steady.

And then—

Noises. Faces. Strangers greeting me by my name.

As he guided me toward a pew, Tom whispered comforting words.

We sat down, but it was too much. Too loud. Too bright. Too many people. Panic swelled inside me. I couldn't think. Couldn't focus.

"I have to leave," I whispered, barely able to form the words.

Tom looked at me with concern. "Why?"

I shook my head and said, "I need to leave. *Now.*"

He took my hand again and we headed toward the exit. On wobbly legs, I made it back to the car.

Exhausted, I collapsed into the seat—shaking, drained.

Will I ever be able to return?

MARY'S INJURY HAD changed everything. There was no map for the road we were on, and the future felt more uncertain with each passing day.

She was a shadow of the vibrant woman she had once been. Even simple tasks remained overwhelming, like choosing clothes to wear and putting them on. She lived in a haze of headaches and confusion, and I lived there with her, trying to be a light for her.

Please God, help me take care of her.

On the bathroom counter, there were twenty-three prescription bottles lined up in rows like little soldiers—an army I managed every day. Mary was far too disoriented to take them on her own, so I had to give them all to her. I counted out pills like they were jewels and made sure I gave her everything exactly right.

I learned she had a sensitive system, easily overwhelmed by the painkillers, opioids. They dulled her pain, but clouded her mind, making it harder for her to think. I told the doctors about her adverse reactions to the opioids and pleaded for alternatives, but they kept saying she needed them. As I continued giving her the pills, I worked hard to keep her mind stimulated with conversation and easy activities.

ONE MORNING, I walked quietly into the bedroom, as sunlight peeked through the curtains. "Hey Mary," I said barely above a whisper, "are you awake?"

No answer.

I smiled at the sight of her sleeping. Dr. Anderson had told me sleeping late was good for her brain—that it helped it heal. It wasn't unusual for her to sleep late, and I left the room.

I glanced into the bedroom a few times later that morning, but she showed no signs of waking.

When noon came, I decided it was time for her to get up. She'd never slept this late.

I moved to her side and patted her arm. "Mary? It's time to get up."

No response.

She was lying on her back. I leaned over, pressing a hand to her shoulder, and gently shook her. "Mary?"

Still nothing.

A sudden wave of alarm surged through me. I grabbed both shoulders and shook her. "MARY! WAKE UP!"

She didn't stir.

Fear gripping me, I rolled her onto her stomach, then back onto her back.

She didn't even move.

Panicked, I yanked my phone from my pocket and punched in 911.

"I NEED AN AMBULANCE! QUICK! My wife's asleep and won't wake up!"

WHEN SHE FINALLY woke in the hospital, her eyes grew wide with confusion.

"Tom, why am I here?"

"You wouldn't wake up this morning. I had to call an ambulance, and they brought you here."

"Whaaat?"

"You wouldn't wake up." I took her hand.

She shook her head. "No, th—"

"Yeah. And the emergency room doctor said it was your fault, that you took your medicine wrong."

She stared at me in disbelief. "Huh?"

"I told him, 'No, she didn't! She took it exactly as prescribed.' Then he asked me, 'How do you know that?' And I told him, 'Because I gave it to her myself!'"

Her face crumpled. "Oh, Tom. I'm so sorry."

I took both of her hands. "Lord, please help us. Mary really needs you now. Please comfort us and help the doctors heal Mary. Lord, we put our trust in you. Amen."

Mary spent the afternoon resting as the medical staff monitored her. One doctor went over all her prescriptions with me and discontinued one of the opioids.

The sun was setting when Mary was finally discharged.

As I helped her into the car, I told her, "I'm going to put Dr. Anderson in charge of all your prescriptions. From now on, everything goes through him. We can't have you get overdosed again."

She nodded, her eyes heavy with exhaustion. I knew she probably wouldn't remember our conversation.

That evening, after she fell asleep, I typed a list of all her medications, then tucked copies into her wallet and mine. I needed to always be ready for the questions anyone asked about them.

I continued giving Mary all her prescriptions every day, hoping she'd be able to stop taking them soon.

No matter how lost she was, no matter how dark the road ahead—I loved her and was determined to take good care of her.

26

The Gears Were Turning

Four Months After

The smell of pepperoni pizza filled the air as I stood in the kitchen putting slices onto plates.

I heard the light pad of Mary's footsteps behind me, and I turned and smiled. "Hey, darling, dinner's ready."

"I love my new ring," she said, lifting her hand between us. Her voice was hesitant. "But I keep bumping it on things."

"Oh?" I glanced at the ring. It looked beautiful on her.

"Why?" I asked.

"It's too big."

I dried my hands on a dish towel and held out my palm. "Okay. Let me see what I can do to fix it."

Her eyes searched mine—uncertain. I could see she was caught between needing to let it go and wanting to keep it on her hand.

I stepped closer, gently closing her fingers in mine.

"Sweetheart," I said, "I'll take care of it. I promise."

Finally, she slipped it off her finger and put it in my palm like it was precious.

"Just give me a little time," I said.

I thought of all the things I needed to get done, all the ways I had to keep helping her—and added the ring to my to-do list.

THROUGHOUT EACH DAY, the gears in Mary's mind were turning, but they weren't clicking into place. Sometimes a spark of clarity returned, but mostly, her thinking remained clouded.

Before the accident, she'd been quick-witted and a great conversationalist. I missed the easy connection we had shared. Occasionally, she would say something that reminded me of the woman she had been before, but those moments were fleeting.

I felt the weight of her TBI on our relationship. Moving forward wouldn't mean returning to who we once were—it couldn't. Her memory was mostly gone, and so was our old life. We had to start over, learning each other again, like strangers discovering a new love. The thought was daunting. Her healing could stretch on for years, and even then, the outcome was uncertain. But I loved her—and I would never stop.

In the midst of all the turmoil, I clung to the knowledge that God was in control.

I CAME ACROSS a blouse in my closet that I didn't remember and felt a curious impulse to slip it on before Tom took me out for another lunch. As I stepped into the bedroom, my fingers smoothed the fabric nervously, hoping he'd like it. I wanted to look nice for him.

I called out to Tom, and when he entered the room, the approving look on his face warmed my heart. He moved closer and pointed to a row of delicate glass bottles on my dresser. Each one was a different color, catching the afternoon sunlight like tiny rainbows.

"Do you know what those are?" he asked.

I shook my head.

He smiled. "Your perfumes."

I stepped closer, eyeing them.

"You used to love wearing them," he said, touching one gently with his finger.

I picked up a slender bottle with a pale rose-colored liquid, uncapped it, and took a cautious sniff. Sweet, floral, elegant. But no memory came.

I tried another. Citrusy and sharp. Still nothing.

Tom stepped forward with a grin and snatched a tall gold bottle, spraying it on my neck before I could spin away. We burst out laughing—warm, carefree laughter that spilled across the room.

"Why'd you do that?" I asked, giggling.

"That," he declared proudly, "is my favorite. It's called 'Beautiful.'"

Still smiling, I tilted my head and asked again, "But why'd you spray me?"

"I love it when you wear that." He stepped closer and gently slid his arm around my waist. "I really do love that perfume on you," he said in a low voice, a playful sparkle in his eyes. "Always have."

The way he said it—casual, yet full of warmth—stirred something deep inside me. Not a memory exactly, but a feeling. Familiar. Safe. Loved.

In that moment, I felt the desire to remember. I picked up the 'Beautiful' and inhaled it slowly. Closing my eyes, I tried to commit the scent to memory.

"I'll wear it again," I said, opening my eyes.

He smiled, pulling me close. "I'm glad. Because it reminds me of you, and I love you."

"Tell me again," I said softly.

"You are the love of my life," he said.

"TOM, DOES THE name Cyndi Miller mean anything to you?" I asked.

He looked at me, puzzled. "No. Why?"

"I don't know. It just keeps coming into my thoughts. I've tried to ignore it, but I can't. I need to know who she is."

He paused a moment, then his face lit up. "Do you remember Ellen? Your friend at work?"

"I ... I'm not sure."

"Let's call your office, and you ask for Ellen. Maybe she'll know."

"Okay."

He told me that my phone was turned off and put away, and he called the office on his and handed it to me.

A woman answered. Her voice sounded familiar.

"Ellen?" I asked.

"Mary! Oh my goodness, it's so good to hear from you. Everyone misses you, and I'm so sorry you won't be coming back to work."

I didn't know how to respond, so I didn't. Instead, I asked about the name.

"Cyndi? Yes, she's the bank manager across the street from our office, and she's your friend."

I closed my eyes and tried to summon up an image of Cyndi or the sound of her voice. Anything. But the name was all I knew.

Ellen gave me her number, and I called her.

"Hi, Cyndi," I started. "This is Mary Parker, and I ... um ... can I ask you, do you know who I am?"

"Mary," she said, her voice full of warmth. "Of course I do. I heard about the accident. I've been thinking of you. How are you?"

It was strange when someone spoke to me like they knew me but I didn't know them.

I explained about her name coming to me.

She was kind, but just as puzzled as I was. We talked for a few minutes, and after we hung up, my confusion lingered.

"Tom, why do I remember the name of someone else, but I barely remember my children?"

His eyes softened, and he pulled me into his arms. "I don't know," he said quietly. "But you're getting better, and that's what matters."

As I leaned into the strength of his arms and the love in his heart, I felt it—a life still waiting for me.

SOMEBODY KNOCKED ON the front door.

When I opened it, a woman I didn't recognize stood there.

"Hi, Mary," she smiled. "It's good to see you."

Flustered, I struggled to reply. "Oh."

"Is Tom here?" she asked.

Tom appeared beside me. "Mary, this is my sister Anna. I'm sorry, Anna, she doesn't remember you. Come on in."

My thoughts had started moving a little faster, but my memory still didn't work much and Anna was a stranger. She seemed friendly, and I wanted to remember her. She stepped inside, handing a dish to Tom, and we all moved into the living room.

As Tom and Anna talked, I pushed myself to follow their conversation, but my mind suddenly spiraled away with half-formed ideas.

Anna's presence was comforting, but I was having a typical bad day and my brain quickly tired out. When she had to leave, she asked, "Is there anything I can do to help you guys?"

We both said no.

I told her, "I hope you'll come back."

"I will," she replied with a smile. "Take good care of each other."

Her words lingered but I didn't know what to make of them.

TOM KEPT TAKING us to meet with our counselor. Each meeting with Cathy felt like a new beginning. As she spoke with me, my thinking slowly started to shift, and I felt a little more hopeful. But I still struggled to make sense of everything happening around me.

As I usually did, I kept asking Tom for help with my thoughts. My mind was increasingly chasing ideas in every direction.

"What can I do?" he asked gently.

"Why do I have this head injury?"

"Because you were in an accident."

"But why did it have to happen to me?"

"Darling, sometimes we don't get the answers to our questions."

Darling. The word caught in my heart. I wasn't sure why he used it, but I liked it.

I kept asking him questions, needing answers.

"Mary, just keep taking things one step at a time," he said.

One step, I told myself. Then the next.

He read to me from the Bible: "I can do all this through him who gives me strength."[1]

As he spoke, I noticed the warmth in his voice and the kindness in his eyes. There was a quiet confidence about him,

---

[1] Philippians 4:13

and his presence drew me. And the way he looked at me—like I was important—stirred a warmth inside me.

"I recall hearing that," I said slowly.

"Ahh, that's good," he replied, his smile reassuring.

Recognizing the verse felt like a victory, and the hope inside me grew a little bigger.

27

Divergent Thinking

Tom scheduled me with a new cognitive therapist, Melinda. She had bright, inquisitive eyes.

She leaned forward, a playful smile on her lips. "What's the first thing that pops into your head when I say 'baseball'?"

"John Smoltz."

She raised her eyebrows, surprised. "Who's that?"

"A pitcher for the Atlanta Braves," I replied, not knowing how I knew it, or anything else about him. It was like the answer had popped into my mind from out of nowhere.

Melinda nodded, then asked another question. "Okay. What comes to your mind when I say ... 'Baskin-Robbins'?"

"Vanilla."

She blinked and looked at me with curiosity. "Vanilla?"

"Yep. Vanilla."

"That's unusual," she said, smiling. "What you're doing is called divergent thinking. It's a way of thinking that finds many possible answers—kind of like creative brainstorming."

"Oh?"

She nodded. "Yes. Most people try to find one answer, step by step, instead of exploring multiple possibilities. But your thinking style is different—it's outside the box. Your mind makes unusual connections. For instance, instead of a certain player, you might have said 'the Atlanta Braves.'"

"All right," I said, my mind whirling with ideas of what that could mean. Realizing I had divergent thinking sent a thrill through me—there was a name for how my mind worked.

"When I said 'Baskin-Robbins,'" she continued, "a typical response might have been 'ice cream'—something general. Not a specific flavor."

I nodded slowly, even as my mind spun from one thought to another.

Was my thinking wrong? The question hit me like a splash of cold water.

I didn't *choose* to think how I did. It just happened. My mind sometimes darted from one idea to the next, while I just tried to keep up.

She smiled encouragingly. "Let's keep going." She kept asking questions and offering insights.

WEEK AFTER WEEK, I met with Melinda, pushing myself to learn what she wanted me to know. But no matter how much I tried, I could only see things one way—black and white. There was no middle ground. My mind dealt in absolutes. Yes or no. On or off. Shades of gray didn't exist for me.

And my literal way of thinking was all I knew.

I told Tom about my conversations with Melinda, asking him about things she'd said, half-hoping he would translate it all for me.

Instead, he encouraged me to keep working with her, listen more closely, and search for the intention behind her words.

I wanted to understand people when they spoke, but their words and ideas often felt out of reach—like riddles I couldn't solve. The harder I tried to figure out how they communicated, the more it felt like I was learning a foreign language.

Lord, please help me think better.

MARY'S CONFUSION WAS ongoing and every day she kept asking questions, including ones she'd asked many times before.

Thank God for our Christian faith. We had talked about it often before the accident, and now, in the midst of our TBI nightmare, it was a source of strength.

Believing that the more I knew about TBI, the better I could help her, I continued searching online to learn everything I could. I learned that brain injuries were like fingerprints— every injury had similarities in common, but every injury was also unique. I learned that after being injured, the brain could rewire itself through something called *neuroplasticity*. It was the brain's ability to grow new neural pathways, enabling it to function in new ways. And I learned that just like a muscle, the brain needed exercise to be healthy.

I was determined to keep working for Mary's recovery, for the new life we were building, and for the Mary of the future.

28

Are These Really My Clothes?

Five Months After

Standing in the closet Tom said was mine, I looked at the hanging clothes—colorful blouses, dresses, skirts, and pants in various patterns and styles. I ran my hand across the fabrics as I bit my lower lip, hoping something would jog my memory. But nothing did.

Maybe I had liked these clothes before. Maybe they had meant something to me once, but now, I couldn't decide.

Getting dressed was always a challenge. I had trouble telling the difference between the back and front of a T-shirt, and often put it on backwards. Or inside-out. It looked the same to me. Buttons and zippers were impossible to get right. The mere thought of dressing myself made me frustrated.

Clothes shouldn't be so hard to put on.

Often, when I thought I'd gotten dressed right, Tom would gently tell me that I needed to fix something. I'd instantly bristle and ask what was wrong. And when he explained, anger at myself rose inside me.

"Tom," I called out, "I don't recognize these clothes. Do I like them?"

He stepped beside me, his presence calming. "You used to. Do you think you like them now?"

"I don't know."

"Would you like to go shopping for clothes?" he asked.

The idea didn't sound difficult, but panic welled up inside me. I swallowed hard and clenched one of the blouses so tightly my knuckles turned white.

Shopping. Can I do it or will it be too much?

Teetering on the edge of indecision, I finally agreed. Almost immediately, regret whispered at me, but it was too late to turn back. I had to try. I couldn't let the injury steal any more of my life. *I've got to try to be strong.*

Tom took me to a store I didn't recognize and said it was where I bought many of my clothes. Inside, my eyes widened as I took in the vast array of clothing. I still saw four of everything, and I didn't know where to start. Worse, I didn't have a clue what I liked.

"Pick out anything you want," Tom encouraged.

"I don't know where to start."

Taking my hand, he led me into the sea of clothes. "This is your favorite department."

Looking around, I felt a pang of loss. None of the clothes held any meaning for me.

"I don't know what I like!"

"That's okay," Tom said. "I'll help you. Let's find something you think looks nice."

I stared at the racks, utterly lost. "But Tom, I don't know how—"

"All right." He took my hand again and led me to a dressing room. "You wait here, and I'll bring some things you might like. You can try them on and see what you think."

As I waited, I realized that my personal taste and sense of style were more things the injury had stolen from me.

Tom returned with clothes.

I picked up a blouse and ran my fingers over it. Taking a deep breath, I slipped it on and studied my reflection in the mirror.

Does it look good? How am I supposed to know?

Slowly, I walked out to show Tom.

"What do you think?" I asked.

He smiled warmly. "Darling, I think it looks pretty on you, but I think everything looks pretty on you. Choose whatever you like."

I appreciated his support, but how could I make him understand I had no idea what I liked anymore? That I couldn't tell what looked good? I looked in the mirror again, feeling dejected. *What difference does it make?*

"Tom, I really don't care what I wear," I sighed.

"Are you sure?"

"I'm sure. I'm tired. I want to go home."

He nodded. "It's okay, darling. We can try another time."

I changed back into my own blouse. At the register, Tom bought two new blouses he thought I would like.

Back home, as I hung the new blouses in the closet, my eyes landed on a group of scrubs in various colors. Suddenly a memory flared. "Tom!"

He hurried into the closet, and I pointed to the uniforms. "I remember those! Those are what I used to wear to work."

A wave of excitement washed through me. *I remember wearing the scrubs!*

Tom grinned. "It's a memory, Mary. That's a good sign."

I knew it was. And as I stood there, I let myself believe that maybe, just maybe, I was finding my way back.

A MAN CAME to our house one afternoon.

Tom said, "Mary, Pastor Paul is here."

Paul sat down in the living room with us, and as he talked, I experienced a sudden jolt of memory.

"I remember your voice!" I exclaimed. "I remember hearing you talk!"

Paul laughed, his eyes crinkling at the corners. "Well, I hope so. I do talk a lot."

"You tell stories," I said with conviction. The memory was so real that I was positive it *was* a memory. It was only a small memory, but in that moment, it felt like hope had opened the door just a bit wider.

"I'm glad you remember me," Paul said. "If I can ever do anything to help you guys, just let me know. And remember, even when you feel lost, God still knows where you are."

We visited a little longer, and he prayed for us before he left.

"CLOSE YOUR EYES," Tom told me with a playful smile, "and no peeking until I say."

I did what he said, trusting him completely, and listened as his footsteps moved behind me. Then something light and cool brushed my neck. *A necklace!* I couldn't wait to see it.

"Okay, open your eyes."

I looked down and saw a pretty gold pendant with colored stones sparkling from a gold chain.

"Do you recognize it?" Tom asked softly, watching my face.

I shook my head. "No."

He took my hand. "A couple of weeks ago, you told me your ring was too big. I took it back to the jeweler and had him cut off the top and turn it into this pendant. Now, darling, every time you look in the mirror and see it, you'll be reminded that the children and I love you."

Thrilled, I reached up to hold the pendant and found that my thumb fit perfectly into a hollow on the back. I squeezed it lightly between my thumb and index finger, delighted.

It felt like my own lucky charm—a piece of love I could wear.

"Oh, Tom, it's beautiful." I beamed up at him. "I love it. Thank you."

His thoughtfulness touched me. As I held the pendant, a warm emotion filled me, and a thought fluttered in my mind— *this man I'm married to is so good to me. I want to know him. Really know him.* Without thinking, I stepped closer and wrapped my arms around him. He held me tightly, as if he never wanted to let me go, his breath warm against my face.

In that moment, nothing else existed. I felt entirely loved. I wanted to hold on to the moment, but even as we embraced, my mind suddenly wandered, and I struggled to recall what had led me to that moment. *What was it?*

My memory was like a piece of tape that had lost its stickiness.

29

The Darkness Continues

My mind held me prisoner in a black hole of memory loss. I still didn't know who I was, and I was starting to believe I never would.

One morning, I woke early and saw through a window that the day outside was still cloaked in darkness, hiding everything, just like the darkness in my mind.

"Tom, why does it matter what time I get up, what I wear, or when I go to bed?"

Because to me, it didn't.

He sat on the edge of the bed. "You just need more time. Try to be patient with yourself."

Throughout each day, fragmented thoughts kept flickering and vanishing before I could catch them. Nothing stayed. Any activity I attempted, however small, required a huge amount of thought, every task a giant challenge.

Guilt sank its claws into me. I hated what I was putting Tom through. My tears, always just beneath the surface, seemed like my only way to cope, and they spilled out frequently.

Tom took me to see Dr. Anderson again. Another diagnosis—depression. Another pill.

My life felt like a disaster. Yet Tom kept acting as if there was hope. Every night, I listened to him pray, asking God to help me heal and give me back my memory. Before sleep pulled me under, he told me he loved me and gave me a gentle kiss.

MARY'S MEMORY REMAINED inconsistent and erratic, like a lightbulb flickering on and off—mostly off. She was still living minute to minute. Her struggles were my struggles, and I poured every ounce of strength I had into keeping her steady. Sometimes I worried it wouldn't be enough.

How can I take care of someone so hurt?

She had become fixated on her TBI, but her attempts to talk about it were too stressful for either of us. Her inability to understand what had happened to her upset her even more than she already was.

Her cognition continued to change and evolve, and as each day presented new developments, I encouraged her to think through them.

I kept working hard to try to turn things around for her, to help her have more good days than bad ones, but it was proving far more difficult than I could have imagined.

More than ever, I knew we needed God to give us the help that only he could give, and I prayed aloud for Mary, holding her hands, every chance I had.

"Lord, thank you for loving us and for being our Lord. Please help Mary get her memory back. We put all our problems and everything else into your hands. Help us to do your will. Amen."

AS I LOOKED out the window one day into the backyard, a rustling behind me drew my attention. I turned around to see Tom.

"Hello, soldier," I said.

His eyes widened. "What did you say?"

"I said, 'Hello, soldier.' You were in the military, remember?" I laughed as he walked toward me, his eyes still wide.

He pulled me up from the chair and wrapped his arms around me. "You remembered!" He grinned.

I leaned into his embrace, enjoying the feel of his warmth. "Remembered what?"

"That I was in the military. Darling, that's wonderful."

What is he talking about?

I pulled away from him. "What's wonderful?" I asked, a confused smile on my face.

"You called me 'soldier.'"

I did? Why did I do that?

"You reminded me I was in the military," Tom said, but as he spoke, the smile faded from his face.

His expression made me sad. I wanted to ease his sorrow, but I didn't understand.

"Why are you sad?"

"You called me 'soldier.' I thought you remembered."

"Remembered what?"

"That I was in the military."

"You were?"

He nodded.

Instead of racking my brain to remember, I instinctively uttered the first thing that came to mind. "Maybe I remembered, but then I forgot. That still means I remembered something, right?"

He looked curiously at me for a moment, then smiled as he hugged me close once more. "That's true," he said. "That's something."

I smiled too and snuggled into his embrace.

TOM PLACED A glass of iced tea on the table beside my recliner—the only place where I felt comfortable aside from bed.

I lifted the glass to my mouth and tilted it. But a sudden rush of cold spilled down my shirt. I froze. I hadn't gotten it all the way to my lips.

"Be careful!" Tom shouted. "Mary, you've *got* to pay attention and stop spilling things!"

"I'm trying!" I yelled back.

He shook his head, exasperated. "You can't keep doing this. You have to try harder." His tone softened, but disappointment hung in the air. "That was a new chair, and now it's ruined from all the spills."

I was furious—at myself, and at him. I sat there, fuming. *Why can't I eat and drink? Why is everything so hard?*

I stood up and stormed out of the room. A few minutes later, I returned in a clean shirt.

Tom looked up, his expression sorrowful. "I'm sorry for raising my voice," he said quietly.

My thoughts and feelings were tangled in a knot, but his apology began to loosen my anger.

"Tom, I appreciate you trying to help me. I know my injury is hard on you too. And I'm sorry I have so many problems."

"Well, everybody has problems."

"What?"

"Think about it. Everybody has problems, everybody's problems are different, and everybody handles their problems differently. The important thing is to face your problems and manage them the best way you can."

As I thought about Tom's words, I reached up and held my necklace, feeling his love.

AT OUR NEXT support group meeting, the leader announced, "Tonight, we'll start in separate rooms—the survivors in one, caregivers in another. Then we'll all come back together for the second half, as one group again. Like always."

A flicker of unease stirred within me. I glanced at Tom, searching his face for reassurance.

He gave my hand a gentle squeeze. "Could be helpful," he murmured.

As I settled into the circle of survivors, one of them grinned. "I have lots of spills," she said, "and I look good in everything I eat."

Laughter rippled through the room. Such a simple, funny comment, but it sparked something inside me—a bubble of joy rising up.

The rest of the meeting was just as encouraging. When I left, I felt lighter ... more hopeful.

Is this how I used to feel? Can I hold onto this feeling?

That night, settled into my recliner, Tom gave me a plate of dinner. But when I tried to eat, the coordination between my thoughts and hands betrayed me again.

My fingers slipped. The plate tilted. Dinner slid down my blouse and landed in my lap.

For a split second, I froze. Then I burst out laughing.

"I look good in everything I eat," I said, grinning.

Tom gave me an odd look.

"I heard another survivor say that at the support group," I explained.

A slow smile spread across his face, and his eyes lit up.

"That's funny, Mary. But more than that, you remembered it. Your memory's getting better."

I blinked, surprised by the warmth blooming in my chest. It hadn't even occurred to me that I'd remembered something—not just a face or a fact, but a moment. A feeling.

So many times, my days had blurred together, full of effort and repetition. Progress had been elusive. Yet now, with food in my lap, Tom smiled at me like I'd just solved a puzzle.

Am I coming back to myself?

THE CHANGES IN Mary were profound.

But even with her topsy-turvy cognition, my lack of sleep, and our accumulating stress, I knew that I had to stay strong for her.

With almost everything she attempted, she took three steps forward, then two or three backward. It was hard to watch. She so badly wanted to get things right that even the smallest mistakes left her frustrated and disheartened.

Still, something had shifted recently. Her attitude about spilling food and drink—something that used to leave her near tears—had lightened. And every so often, a flicker of humor surfaced, as if a part of her were quietly finding its way back.

Yet the persistent challenges of the TBI made each day feel like walking a tightrope in the dark. One moment she would be laughing; the next, without warning, her expression would cloud over as confusion or anger swept through her.

Lord, Mary's brain injury is really hard. It's too much. I know you think I can do all this, but I know I can't. I need your help. If you will just give her back to me enough that I can recognize her as my wife from before the accident, I will go wherever you want me to go and do whatever you want me to do, for the rest of my life, no questions asked.

30

"Let's Start Again"

Tom sat down beside me on the couch. "Hey, would you like to go on a lunch date?"

A tender note in his voice brushed against my heart like a forgotten melody, stirring something vulnerable inside me.

I blinked. *A date?*

"Darling," he murmured, his eyes searching mine, "don't you remember? We loved going on dates."

"No," I said, my voice hesitant.

He smiled gently. "Then let's start again. It'll be fun."

Start again. The words seemed like a gift, waiting for me to open it. "All right," I murmured.

The look in his eyes stirred something inside me.

"Why don't you wear one of your new blouses?" he asked.

I went to my closet and pulled one of them from the hanger—a soft, sky-colored fabric that sparkled faintly. When I stepped into the living room, his expression lit up.

"I'm ready, Tom."

He stood up and gazed at me with open admiration. "You look beautiful," he said. "And you remembered I love blue."

My heart fluttered. *Did I? Was that why I'd chosen it?*

"I don't know," I admitted softly.

But one thing I knew for sure—I wanted to wear more blue.

THE CAR HUMMED quietly as we pulled away from home, wrapped in the golden glow of sunlight. As the world slipped past outside the window, my pulse quickened at the thought of going on a date with him.

We drove to a small Mexican restaurant, where the rich scent of spices wrapped around us as we stepped inside.

"Do you remember this place?" he asked, his eyes soft and curious, seeking mine.

I let my gaze wander over the bright colors. Cheerful music filled the air.

"I don't recognize anything," I confessed.

"That's okay," he said. "This is one of our favorite places. We used to come here about twice a month. Maybe today we can make a new memory."

At our table, the waitress handed us menus and left. I stared at the pages, unable to read them, my hands trembling slightly.

"What do I like to eat?" I whispered.

He smiled reassuringly. "Lots of things. Just choose anything you want."

"But I don't know what I want!" my frustration spilled out before I could stop it. "And I can't read this."

He leaned over and pointed in my menu. "Look at the pictures and choose something that looks good."

Everything felt strange and familiar at the same time.

"I don't know how to order," I murmured.

"When the waitress comes back, just point to a picture and tell her that's what you want," he said. "It'll be easy."

I was still puzzled, but when the waitress returned, I pointed to a picture of something covered with red sauce. When my food arrived, it smelled delicious, and I couldn't help but smile.

"It's a beef burrito," Tom said softly.

I didn't know if I'd ever had one before, but as I took my first bite, flavor exploded in my mouth, and I felt a satisfying thrill, happy with my choice.

During lunch, Tom talked about how a brain injury could cause a survivor to have difficulty making decisions. And he said that some of them were more important than others.

"I'm not sure I understand," I replied.

He smiled and gently said, "It's okay. What you choose to wear or eat are simple choices you don't need to think about much, but other choices require more thought."

On the drive home, he asked, "When it's hard to make a decision, does that mean making one is wrong?"

The question felt like a riddle. "I don't know."

"There are good, better, and best decisions," he said, glancing at me. "But when one needs to be made, difficult or not, it must be made. When you need to make one but feel you can't, it's all right sometimes to stop, take a break, and come back to it later. And when you avoid making a decision, you're still making one, just a different kind."

I wanted to be able to make decisions again. But I didn't trust myself to. Just the idea felt too enormous.

He asked more questions: What made me happy? What did I want? What would help me recover? What would make my life better?

My head whirled. I had no answers—only the soft ache of wanting to understand.

When we reached home, I wanted to talk more, but I was worn out. My brain had to shut down and rest. I collapsed onto the couch and fell fast asleep.

I GENTLY PLACED a blanket over her, happy we'd been able to go on a date, but sorry it had been so hard for her.

I turned to prayer again. It gave me hope.

God, Mary is hurt so bad, please help us. Keep me strong for her and help me know what she needs to heal. I give you all our problems and trust you to watch over us. And God, please help her start remembering more.

WALKING WAS STILL a big challenge.

Dizziness clung to me. Each step felt uncertain. I didn't trust my balance, and I kept falling, landing on my sore knees.

Everywhere we went, Tom held my hand and pointed out trip hazards as we walked.

He took me to a neuro-ophthalmologist for a comprehensive vision exam.

The doctor said, "The pain happening behind your eyes is called an optic migraine."

I stared at him. "Why do I see four of everything?"

"You have a visual disorder from your brain injury, maybe damage to the optic nerve."

"Will it go away?" I asked.

"It might," he said quietly. "I'll prescribe glasses for you that contain prisms to reduce the multiple images."

AFTER THE VISION appointment, we stopped at Cracker Barrel for lunch.

When lunch was over, as we headed toward the exit, the room began to spin. I cried out as I fell. The last thing I knew, Tom was grabbing me.

I opened my eyes and saw Tom kneeling beside me, and several people peering down at us. Mortified, I wished I could disappear.

"She's okay," Tom told everyone.

"Everyone falls sometimes," he whispered. "We just need to get back up."

I couldn't wait to leave.

MARY'S FAINTING SPELLS kept happening. I prayed it would stop, for both our sakes.

When she sensed one was coming and cried out, I tried to reach her in time—to catch her, cradle her head on the way down so it didn't get hit again, and cushion her fall. But I couldn't be with her every minute.

Too often, the sound came from another room—her sharp cry, or a dull thud. I would find her on the floor. She fell so often she'd grown used to it. But for me, each fall was agony, afraid she'd be injured again.

TOM TOOK ME to me to see Dr. Anderson for a follow-up appointment. When he finished the exam, he left the room.

I stood up to leave. "The room's spinning!"

Tom lunged forward, his arms outstretched.

I woke on the floor—Tom beside me.

"What happened?" I whispered.

"You fell. Come on, let's get you back on your feet."

I started pushing up and winced. "Ouch. My wrist." *Darn it. I hope I didn't break something.*

His brow furrowed. "Isn't that the wrist you broke in the car accident?"

"I don't remember." An ache pulsed through my hand and I rubbed it gingerly.

"Is it okay?"

"I think so."

As we sat there, Dr. Anderson suddenly appeared in the doorway, wide-eyed. "What happened?"

"She passed out," Tom said, "like she often does."

I was embarrassed and wanted to get away as fast as possible. My pride hurt worse than my wrist.

MARY'S LEFT KNEE began to hurt too much for her to want to walk. She tried to hide it, but I could see the pain.

I took her to an orthopedist, who ordered an X-ray. It showed the cartilage in her knee was so damaged from her falls that getting a total knee replacement was the only option.

The surgery was scheduled.

ONE AFTERNOON, I remembered I had two sisters living in Atlanta.

"Tom, I don't recall Meghan or Lorraine ever talking with me since my accident."

He looked at me with gentleness. "They visited you in the hospital," he reminded me. "But you're right, they haven't called since then."

I didn't understand. "Why not?"

"I don't know."

I frowned. "But they're my sisters."

He wrapped his arms around me. "Mary," he said softly, "I don't know what other people are doing, but I know this— you're making real good progress, and whatever happens, I love you. I am so proud of you."

In his embrace, I felt the steady comfort of a man who would never let me go, and I loved how it made me feel.

WHEN WE SAW Dr. Anderson again, he inquired about Mary's fainting, and I updated him.

He sent her to the hospital for an EEG to test the functioning of her brain. The results showed that unusual electrical activity was happening.

I questioned him about what that meant.

He sighed. "It's part of the TBI," he said. "The brain is unpredictable."

I nodded. *Unpredictable.* There was no promise, no timeline, nothing to hold on to. Only faith and the hope that somehow Mary would keep healing.

I WORE THE new prism glasses for two weeks, trying to believe they would help. But looking through them was distorting, and I couldn't handle it. Setting them aside, I returned to my old glasses, resigned to just accept seeing multiple images. I had learned that the image on the far-right side was the real one, and dealing with that was more manageable than seeing distorted images.

What I wanted most wasn't clarity of vision—I longed for memories I could trust, pieces of myself I could keep without them slipping away. Even when I felt sure a fragment had come back, it usually dissolved quickly. It seemed that the harder I tried to remember, the more fragile my memory was.

I questioned Tom about our past again. He patiently began telling more stories, his voice gentle and steady, like a familiar sound guiding me home. His words stirred faint memories—laughter we once shared, times with the children, watching a sunset together. I grasped at those moments, but mostly they kept slipping away.

"TOM, I REMEMBER something about the accident."

His eyes met mine. "Oh?"

"There was a crash, and then a bright light. I walked down a hallway, and I saw my dad and someone else."

"What else do you remember?"

"Someone in the light told me to do something. It felt important, but I don't remember what it was."

A smile pulled at his lips. "Well, that's okay. If you remember more, that's fine; if not, that's fine too. Let me know if you remember anything else, okay darling?"

He drew me gently into his arms as if I were the most precious thing in the world, and a comfort spread through me, soothing the ache of my lost memories. My arms rested lightly around him, a quiet warmth humming through me.

Deep inside, something irresistible was unfolding—my feelings for him were growing.

31

Dr. Strider

Six Months After

Tom reminded me that right after the accident, while I was still in the hospital, he had found a neuropsychologist for me to see. We went to our first appointment with him.

In the lobby, I sat with my hands clasped together, feeling apprehensive, nerves twisting inside me. I didn't like not knowing what would happen.

Tom reached over, covered my hands with his, and whispered, "Darling, you don't need to be nervous. I'll be with you the whole time."

I took a deep breath, comforted by his reassurance.

A man in his mid-fifties stepped through a door. He had brown-rimmed glasses, kind eyes, a white shirt, blue tie, dark slacks, and shiny black loafers.

"Hello, Mary," he said warmly. "I'm Dr. Strider. It's very nice to meet you."

He led us into a quiet office, the faint scent of coffee hanging in the air. His voice was calm as he asked me how my memory was working.

I told him it mostly gave me scattered fragments, and I couldn't tell how—or even if—they connected, but that sometimes, a larger piece of memory would appear for a moment. My memory faltered at many of his questions, leaving me blank and silent.

Fatigue pulled at me, and the silence between us widened until Tom began filling in the answers. The more Dr. Strider pressed for details, the more I relied on Tom to provide the information. Desperate to remember the details of my life, I tried to focus on what he told the doctor.

Then came the testing. Dr. Strider placed a jigsaw puzzle on the desk—an elephant, with ten pieces, and told me to connect them. My eyes searched, my hands moved, but no matter how hard I tried, the picture refused to come together.

Frustration and defeat welled inside me, and I sighed heavily.

"Don't worry about it," Dr. Strider said. "Remember, 'with God all things are possible.'² And in time, you may be able to do what seems impossible now."

I sighed again.

"You shouldn't be frustrated. Your brain is still healing. It could take a long time for it to get better," Dr. Strider said.

I wanted my memory back immediately, and hearing it would take more time felt unbearable. I stared at the doctor, trying to understand.

---

² Matthew 19:26

He smiled and acted encouraging. "Where you are today is not where you're going to be later. Just let things happen in their own time. Don't try to force anything. And if you can write things down, it'll help you."

Impossible. I can't even read. How can I write?

At a loss, I looked at Tom.

He smiled and took my hand. "Darling, we can do this."

The word "we" sparked hope inside me.

He said we can, so I want to believe.

Dr. Strider nodded. "If you can write about the injury and how you feel, it'll help you heal and improve your memory."

"This will be a big challenge for her, Doc," Tom said, "but I'll try to help her."

Dr. Strider nodded approvingly. "Having a positive attitude is key in your recovery, Mary. People who are negative do not make as much progress as those who are positive."

I felt reluctant to believe him. How could I be positive when everything was so hard?

After several visits with Dr. Strider, he told us he had enough information to write a psychological evaluation.

"Tom, I'll mail the report to you. And if you have any questions, please don't hesitate to call me."

Dr. Strider shook our hands and wished us well.

"DARLING, WE USED to go on a dinner date every weekend," Tom said one Friday afternoon.

"We did?"

"Yes," he said with a smile. "And we loved it. We always looked forward to it."

"Really?"

"Would you like to have a dinner date with me tonight?"

I smiled shyly. "Okay."

He grinned, and a feeling flickered inside me that I didn't understand, like a half-remembered dream I wanted to have again.

That evening, despite the usual injury challenges, Tom guided me gently through our date. At the restaurant, he helped me get settled, suggested a meal, and recounted stories from our past. I listened closely, drinking in his laughter and the way his eyes lit up, feeling a quiet thrill at being with him.

Arriving home, the car rolled to a gentle stop in the driveway. Tom turned to me, his voice soft. "This was a lot of fun, darling."

Inside, the door clicked shut behind us. Tom paused, then turned, his eyes searching mine. Without a word, he drew me into his arms. His lips brushed mine in a kiss so tender it stole my breath, and I melted against him. The world fell away. I wanted him to do it again, my heart pounding.

He chuckled gently, as if reading my thoughts. "We should do more of this."

My answer was quiet, but sure. "We should." I hoped he knew I meant the kiss as much as the date.

His eyes closed for a moment, and when they opened again, there was a look of hope in his gaze. "Let's go to our room," he said.

A strange flutter of excitement rose through me and my pulse quickened. I smiled and nodded. When he reached for my hand, I slid mine into his and our fingers laced together. We moved toward the bedroom, each step drawing us closer, and quietly shut the door.

32

Deep in the Maze

I pulled a pitcher from the refrigerator and poured a glass of tea, thinking of Tom. When he held me, I felt good—wanted, loved. And when he kissed me ...

A memory struck.

Bang! Rolling—slam—crashing—moving down a hallway of light. A warm feeling of love enveloped me. I saw my dad. And Jesus. I spoke to them. Jesus said—

Like a bubble popping, the memory vanished.

I clutched the counter, chasing the lost words. *What did Jesus say?*

I found Tom and spilled everything in a breathless rush. "I just remembered that I saw Jesus in my near-death experience, and that he spoke to me!"

He stepped closer. "What did he say, Mary?"

"I ... I don't know."

He brushed a thumb over my cheek. "Your memory is getting better. Let it come in its own time."

I THOUGHT OF my past with Mary—of the relationship we'd once had—and a clear picture rose, a scene from two weeks before the accident.

Mary in the kitchen. Moving with a song on her lips, putting the finishing touches on lunch.

"You always get so excited, darling," I teased her. "It's one of the things I love about you."

We'd already straightened the house for company. The table was set with china and a fresh flower arrangement.

A knock at the door. "Hello! Anyone home?" Dylan called out from the hallway. He walked into the kitchen grinning, arms open.

"Hi, Mom and Dad. Smells amazing in here."

Cody and Beth followed right behind, their faces bright.

We wrapped our arms around all the kids, hugging them close.

Beth smiled warmly. "Thank you for having me. It's always nice to be here."

"Of course, Beth," Mary said. "You're part of the family now."

The house filled with chatter, mingling with the comforting smells of roast chicken and warm rolls.

"So, how's Leo doing?" Dylan asked.

"He's good," Mary said. "We talked to him last night. He and Donna love living in Oklahoma." She paused, then asked, "How're the wedding plans coming?"

"I can't believe how many decisions have to be made." Beth smiled. "But it's exciting."

"If there's anything Mary and I can do to help, just let us know," I said.

"We've been looking at venues, Mom, like you recommended," Cody said. "If you want, we'd love you to come look with us. Beth asked her mom to come too."

Mary smiled. "You just let me know when and where, and I'll be there. It'll be fun."

After lunch, we drifted to the living room. Mary pulled out some family photo albums, and we all laughed at early pictures of the boys. The rest of the afternoon flew by.

Too soon, the kids were ready to leave. Mary loaded leftovers into plastic containers for the kids, and they gave us warm hugs at the door.

On the porch, Mary and I waved as the kids drove away, our hearts full. She leaned into me with a soft sigh. "We did good, didn't we?" she asked.

I slid my arm around her. "Yes, we did, darling."

Now, replaying that memory, I felt the ache of everything that had changed—and was reminded how faith, hope, and love were the answer.

MARY KEPT STRUGGLING through the maze of TBI, fluctuating between bad days and better ones.

That evening, as she sat in her recliner, she dropped her fork—then the plate. Food spilled everywhere. She cried out, "Tom, life is too hard! I can't do it anymore!" Tears streamed down her face.

Her despair cut through me. "Darling, I love you. And you can either choose to try, or choose to give up. I know it's hard, but I need you to try. Please."

She gave a long trembling sigh, and a reluctant nod. But her resolve was fragile. Even the simplest activities—being present, talking, walking—remained battles she fought every day. And I fought them with her.

TOM KEPT TAKING me back to the grocery store. One day he convinced me to drive the electric cart.

I made it halfway down the first aisle before frustration consumed me. I told Tom I couldn't drive it—mad at myself for being unable to, and mad at him for asking me to. He didn't argue, just brought me a push basket instead. I clung to the handle like a lifeline.

He handed me a piece of paper with words on it. He said it was a grocery list and told me to try reading it. I stared at the paper, nothing making sense. He took it back and told me what it said. I looked for the items on the shelves but couldn't find anything. Then he said he would find the items, and I could put them in the basket. That worked better.

His eyes lit up and he said, "The store has flowers for sale. I want to buy you some."

I blinked. "Why?"

He stepped closer, brushing my hand with his. "Because you love it when I give you flowers. You made beautiful arrangements, and you can do it again."

A single word escaped me. "Oh."

Then, like a spark catching fire, a memory flared—red roses in a white vase, my hands arranging them. Joy flooded me, warm and bright. *This memory is real!*

I looked up at Tom, stunned by gratitude. With one small gesture, he had reached across the silence in my mind and pulled something from the shadows. A memory, clear and vivid. I was thankful he knew the woman I'd been before.

WHEN IT CAME to daily household tasks, I couldn't rely on Mary. Just trying to talk with her about them increased our stress too much. With a quiet ache, I shouldered everything alone. I missed her—the woman who had once shared every plan, every choice, every corner of my life. I missed the pleasant warmth and joy she had carried every day. Her TBI remained a mystery to her, me, and her doctors, and I prayed she'd keep healing.

I read everything I could about TBI. One article mentioned a test called a PET scan. At Mary's next neurology appointment, I asked about it. Dr. Murphy ordered the scan, and at our next appointment, she said the results showed Mary had irregular brain activity.

"What does that mean?" I asked.

Dr. Murphy looked at me with a solemn expression. "Her brain is processing information differently than normal."

It wasn't something I wanted to hear, but I already knew that certain mannerisms and ways she'd spoken before were gone. Every action, every thought, even the simplest tasks now bore the marks of her injury—a stark contrast to how easily she'd once done them.

I wanted that ease to come back. For her. For us.

I hoped the scan results would help the doctors better understand and treat her condition.

A LETTER FROM my mom arrived, her first contact since I'd come home from the hospital. As I held the envelope, my mind raced, imagining what might be inside.

Since I couldn't read, Tom read it to me. Mom was home in Oklahoma and apologized for not reaching out sooner. She said she loved us, asked about my progress, and wanted one of us to call her.

I had Tom read it to me again. Slowly. Then I called her.

The conversation felt awkward. A few memories of our relationship surfaced, but there was too much I didn't remember. I couldn't understand why we didn't seem close. All I could guess was that I didn't know the whole story.

After the call, I thought about the distance between Mom and me.

Lord, please help me remember my past with Mom. Heal my relationship with her. Help us grow close again.

A murky echo surfaced. A long-past disagreement—hurt feelings on both sides, a rift that never healed before the accident. It suddenly returned in a flash.

As I thought about everything, a wave of discomfort washed over me. My memories were still tangled, some of them broken fragments, others sharp and painful. But one thing was sure: the distance between me and others felt impossibly wide.

33

Denial

I sat at the kitchen table, morning sunlight slanting through the window, trying not to spill my coffee. Tom sat down across from me and spoke gently.

"Darling, we need to talk. The TBI has hurt you more than you realize."

I didn't respond.

He sighed, his expression filled with concern. "Mary, I know this isn't easy, but I'm worried. You've been denying the truth, and acting like you're not."

"Oh?" I glanced at him.

His gaze softened. "Yes. You're shutting out that you got hurt in the ways you did. But denial and pretending make things worse."

"I don't like what happened."

"Remember yesterday, when you said the waitress got your order wrong?"

"She did."

"I'm sorry, darling, but you forgot what you said you wanted. She gave you what you asked for, and you got frustrated at her. I know it's difficult to understand, but you need to."

I hate the mistakes I'm making. I wanted to shove them out of my mind and pretend they'd never happened.

"Mary," he said quietly, "denying the truth causes more problems. And you keep getting upset because you're not facing things and understanding. Are you listening?"

"That's hard to take in."

"I know, sweetheart. But just because you want something to be true doesn't make it true."

Am I blocking myself from recovery?

"Mary, denial is your enemy. It only holds you back. You need to realize that. Do you understand?"

"I think so." I was willing to do anything to get better.

"The more honest you are, the more you can heal. But holding onto denial makes it harder. Can you see that?"

"I guess." *I hate the injury!* I rubbed my temples, willing myself to understand what Tom said.

He continued quietly. "I'm sorry you're hurt, darling, but you need be honest, about everything."

"I understand."

"That's good," he said. "Admitting the problems will open the door for more recovery. I want to give you some time to think about this. It's very important, so I'm going to go work in the office."

I watched him walk away, trying to press what he'd said into my memory. But my thoughts drifted. I loved Tom—his smile, the warmth of his arms around me, the comfort of his presence. He was only in the other room, but I already missed him. My memories of our life before the accident remained mostly out of reach, but I wanted to be the wife he needed.

I SAT AT my desk sipping a glass of tea, thinking about Mary. I knew that for her to heal more, she had to face the truth of what had happened. And I had to find more ways to help her understand.

Lord, please help me know what to tell Mary and how to say it. I'm sorry I have so many problems, but I love her and want to help her. Thank you.

At times, Mary's thinking was clearer, but other times, it still seemed like she hadn't recovered much. It was hard to see the progress she was making, but I knew she was moving in the right direction. Still, her new ways of thinking puzzled me. How could she have her new ability to hear all the parts in a song, yet struggle with so many other things?

I set my glass on the desk, my eyes drawn to the paper beside it. The letter from Mary's mom prompted me to respond in kind, since Mary had forgotten how to write. I hoped my letter could help close the distance between us.

I updated her on Mary's progress. "I love Mary, and I'm taking good care of her," I wrote. I thanked her for raising such a good, loving woman, and finished the letter with an open invitation to come visit anytime, adding, "Mary and I would love to see you."

I RARELY SAW Dylan and Cody. Tom said we had been close to them before the accident, and that they lived nearby.

"Tom, why don't they come see me more?"

He paused before answering. "I guess they're busy."

"But they could still come see me."

"I know, Mary. They did a few times, just not recently. You must've forgotten."

"But Tom, I want to see them. And they've got memories that would help me."

He nodded. "You're right. And I've called and encouraged them to stay in touch." His expression turned solemn. "I'm sorry, Mary."

"There must be a reason they're staying away," I said.

They would visit if they could, wouldn't they?

Tom always took time to talk with me, so his not answering sent a whisper of concern through me. "What are the boys doing?"

"I don't know, darling."

I shook my head.

"Mary, I'm doing everything I can to take care of you, your appointments, and our house. I'm hoping the boys will come by soon."

The boys' absence made me feel anxious, and I couldn't stop thinking about them. I pushed my mind as hard as I could, and a faint memory of their childhood surfaced. Christmas with the boys in matching pajamas, their opening gifts with happy grins.

"You know, Mary," Tom said, "you should call the two boys, tell them you miss them. See what they're up to. Let them know you want them to come visit."

I called the boys, asking them to come over the next weekend. They said they were busy. I tried to figure out what they were doing, but it taxed my mind. Sometimes they did come see me, but their visits were always too short.

Lord, thank you for my children. Please help them make good decisions and come back to me.

AN ENVELOPE FROM Dr. Strider arrived in the mail— the neuropsychological evaluation he had written about Mary. I read it practically holding my breath, hoping it would shed new light on the injury.

The report was thorough—twelve pages of clear, clinical insight. It confirmed some of the problems I'd been guessing at and revealed others I hadn't realized. I was grateful for the information it provided, but it was too discouraging to share with Mary. I filed it away for the future.

The bottom line remained the same—I loved Mary, and now, armed with Dr. Strider's report, I was better equipped to help her.

Mary continued to experience big swings of emotional and cognitive volatility, and she was very impulsive. She hadn't been like that before the accident. I prayed God would give me patience when her struggles flared up, and I kept believing she would continue to heal.

MY HEAD THROBBED from pushing myself to figure out things I didn't understand. Sometimes when I tried, it seemed like there was something inside my mind blocking me, and I wanted to get past it.

Is my mind hiding things from me?

Wanting to fill the gaps in my thoughts, I spilled my frustration to Tom, asking for his help again. "Why can't I understand things better?"

He sighed. "Mary, if you would just accept things the way they are, your life, and mine, would be much easier. But you keep avoiding the truth. And it's causing more problems. For both of us. Don't you see that?"

Anger burst out of me before I could stop it. "You don't understand!" I shouted. "I HATE what happened to me!"

"Don't yell at me!" he snapped, his voice rising. He paused, taking in a deep breath, and when he spoke again, his tone had softened. "I know you do. But you need to be honest about everything."

Why doesn't he know I'm trying?

"And you've got to stop denying that you're in denial. That doesn't work."

TOM WALKED INTO the living room, holding out the phone. "Hey, Mary," he said, "someone's on the phone who wants to talk to you."

I took it from him, eyebrows raised. "Hello?"

"Hi, Sis. How've you been doing?"

I recognized his voice the moment he spoke.

"Joe! It's so good to hear from you." I couldn't help the smile that spread across my face.

"I've been thinking about you guys," he said. "How are things coming along?"

What a big question. "The injury's really hard, but I think I'm getting a little better."

"I'm glad to hear it. I can't imagine what things have been like."

Maybe he can help me remember?

"Actually, I've got some questions about our childhood."

"Sure. What do you want to know?"

"When we were growing up, didn't Mom and Dad have an apple tree in the backyard?"

He chuckled. "Nope. We had a peach tree. Mom used to cook with those things all the time. Everyone in the family ended up hating peaches."

"A peach tree, hmm ..." I repeated, trying to commit it to memory. "Okay. What about this? Didn't we live on a street where there were lots of other kids?"

"That's right. There were kids living all around Mom and Dad's house outside Oklahoma City."

"And didn't we have a brown dog there named Ginger?"

"There was a dog named Ginger, but not at that house. It was at Mom and Dad's previous house."

"Hmm. Okay."

"You got part of it right," Joe said. "You're getting better, and that's what matters."

"Thanks, Joe." I smiled, grateful for his encouragement.

"How's your family?" I asked.

"We're all good. I've been riding my motorcycle a lot."

Concern passed through me. "Be careful."

"I will, Sis. I love you. Call me anytime, okay?"

I said I would, and we hung up.

As I sat there, reflecting on the call, I realized my memory was getting better. Like with the dog, Ginger—it was a solid, real memory. I'd gotten a detail wrong, but the memory was still a win. It was small, but every win mattered.

34

Lunch Dates

Eight Months After

Although the TBI still loomed over Mary like a dark cloud, she was slowly returning to me, like a flame being rekindled.

I'd begun replacing our fast-food outings with dates to quiet restaurants where servers waited on tables. These dates gave Mary the opportunity to practice handling new experiences in a calm setting, and I continued expressing how much I loved her. I encouraged her to focus on positive thoughts—the pleasant surroundings, the friendly service, the fun of being on our date. During this time, I could feel her coming back to me.

I CHANGED OUR counselor from Cathy to someone who specialized in the unique challenges of brain injury. It gave Mary a fresh beginning from which to share her thoughts and receive feedback. And we continued attending the TBI support group.

I was often surprised by the "new" Mary—her thoughts and personality were much different from before the accident. I kept engaging her mind by involving her in little tasks and taking her on errands, challenges that pushed her to think and grow.

NINE MONTHS AFTER the accident, Dylan appeared at our home unexpectedly. He'd been distant since the accident, but we were glad to see him. I thought maybe he had finally come to offer help.

When the accident first happened, I had made a point of calling all three children regularly, updating them on Mary's condition. Leo lived too far away to visit us, and the other boys hadn't come around much. But over time, those calls became impossible—Mary's needs were too critical for me to spend time on the phone.

Dylan sat across from Mary in the living room. "I'm sorry I haven't been around more," he said.

We smiled at him, forgiving him instantly. Mary's eyes twinkled with joy. He cleared his throat.

"So ... I, uh, want your help with something," he said.

"What?" Mary said in surprise.

He hesitated a moment before explaining that he wanted to attend a mechanic school in another state and needed our financial support.

Just like that, the smile left Mary's face.

We would do anything we could for him, but Mary's condition had overwhelmed us. I looked him squarely in the eyes. "Dylan, you know Mom has a serious brain injury and needs help, right?"

He nodded. "Yes, but I want this, and I can't do it without your help."

Mary's gaze jumped from Dylan to me and back again, confusion growing in her eyes.

"When does the school start?" I asked.

"Two months from now," he replied.

"How long does it last?"

"A year."

I thought for a moment. "If we help you with your finances, will you come stay with us for two weeks after school ends, so Mom can have some time with you?"

Dylan didn't hesitate. "Yes, I will."

I agreed to give him our help.

I WAS LIVING a life that felt surreal.

Every day, I fought to remember who I'd been before the accident. Fractured memories continued to come and go, filling me with a mix of relief and loss. My confusion was constant, but something had begun to change—I was getting better at handling small tasks that once felt impossible. And I noticed my thinking was getting a little faster.

Out of the blue, a memory came back from a book I'd once read. I couldn't recall the title, but I remembered the message: *Bad things happening to good people didn't mean they'd done something wrong.*

I shared it with Tom, my voice tentative.

His eyes brightened. "That's wonderful," he said warmly.

I felt my spirit lighten, and my hope grew.

LONELINESS TUGGED AT me like a heavy weight. I wanted the company of others, but I didn't know how I could bring anyone into the strange place my mind now called home. I could barely handle it myself.

I told Tom how lonely I was.

"I'm sorry, darling," he murmured. "Would you like to try going back to church? Maybe see your friends there?"

It sounded appealing, but felt outside my reach.

"No, I can't."

"Are you sure?"

"Yes."

He quietly asked, "Can I read you a scripture?"

I nodded.

"Cast your cares on the Lord and he will sustain you."[3]

I smiled softly. When everything felt too difficult, scripture helped give me peace.

"Our faith is important, darling," Tom said. "You know as well as I do that God can do anything. Just be patient. You're getting better."

THE NEXT TIME I spilled my feelings of loneliness to Tom, he asked, "What can I do?"

---

[3] Psalm 55:22

I burst into tears. "The injury is too difficult!"

He wrapped me in his arms. "Mary, I know you can do this. Everything is going to be okay. Just give yourself more time. I need you to get through this. I need you."

I looked up at him through my tears. "How? How can you need me? My life is all messed up! My memory keeps coming and going—I can't remember things!"

His eyes softened and he reached for my hands. "Trust me, Mary. I need you. I love you. You can do this."

I shook my head. "I can't. It's too hard."

He took a deep breath.

"Darling, if you never get any better than you are right now, you're good enough for me."

With his fingers, he tenderly wiped away my tears, then gently pulled me close again, his embrace the only solid thing in my world. I had no idea how he could still want me with my injury.

But if he won't give up on me, how can I give up on myself?

"I need you," he whispered again, his voice filled with certainty. He kissed my cheek. "Please, darling, please keep trying. I'll help you more."

He squeezed me again, his arms tight around me, as though anchoring me to him.

I couldn't bring myself to say it out loud, but his love and belief in me made me want to keep trying.

Tom held my hands and prayed, "God, please help us get through this. Please help Mary's thinking get better. We put everything in your hands and pray for your will. We trust you to be with us and lead us. Thank you for loving us. Amen."

His prayer settled in my mind. Even though I wasn't the same woman he had married, his love made me feel like I still mattered.

I reached up and touched the necklace he'd given me, comforted. As my thumb slid behind the pendant and pressed it against my finger, the hope inside me stirred.

Maybe, just maybe, I wasn't completely lost.

MARY FELT SO cut off from other people that I took her to the local mall to mingle in the crowd. I also thought that window shopping would distract her thoughts from the TBI.

For me, it felt like a little slice of normalcy, but Mary didn't remember ever having been there. The noise, bright lights, and bustle of people overwhelmed her, and with her stamina diminishing rapidly, our venture was short-lived. Still, I saw her reactions and effort to understand things around her as sure signs she was making progress, and knew I would bring her back.

"MARY, I HAVE a job I need you to do."

"What is it?" she asked curiously.

"Can you remember to go to the mailbox each day and get the mail? You did that before the injury, and if you can do it again, it'll be helpful."

She paused, then gave a small nod. "Okay."

"Good. When you bring it inside, I need you to put it on my desk." I led her into the office and pointed to a tray. "Can you remember to put it here?"

She smiled and nodded again. I knew this could be a good step in her recovery, but I also knew it would be a big challenge.

I STOOD AT the kitchen sink, holding a flower arrangement Tom had bought me in one hand, a steak knife in the other. I wanted to put a hole in the bottom of the plastic pot for water to drain out.

I pressed the knife's tip into the base, feeling the plastic giving way. But then, the knife suddenly slipped. A sharp pain shot through my hand and I cried out as the knife clattered into the sink.

Tom burst into the kitchen, his eyes locking on mine immediately. My hands were clenched tightly, blood staining them. He took in the scene with a quick glance, and without a word, yanked a dishtowel from a drawer, quickly covering my hand.

"I was cutting a hole in the bottom of the pot for water—" I started, but before I could say more, he was hustling me to the car. I gripped the towel tightly, my mind racing as he sped toward the emergency room.

"Mary, you've GOT to be careful!" Tom said as we walked into the ER. I couldn't bring myself to answer. I felt guilty, and the pain was starting to pulse. Before long, my hand was stitched up and bandaged.

As we made our way down the hallway toward the hospital exit, I saw a man and woman approaching, in matching uniforms. They stopped, their eyes staring at us for a beat too long before they leaned together, whispering behind their hands. Then they stepped forward, their faces lighting up with excitement.

The woman pointed directly at me. "I remember you!"

"What?" Tom and I said in unison, both of us caught off guard.

"We were the ambulance crew who rescued you after your highway accident," she said, her voice filled with awe. She put a hand to her mouth, her eyes wide. "I ... we didn't think you were going to make it. But you're okay! Oh, wow, you're okay."

"Really?" Tom asked. "You were her crew?"

The man smiled and nodded enthusiastically. "Yes, we were. It's good to see you made it, ma'am. You're looking great."

The woman beside him echoed the sentiment. "Yes, you do!"

Tom and I thanked them for what they'd done that day.

As we stepped out of the ER, I realized that without those two people, I might not have survived.

I TRIED TO remember to get the mail each day, but more often than not, Tom had to remind me. One afternoon, he asked if I'd picked it up that day. I thought I had and told him so, but I wasn't sure.

When he didn't find it on his desk, he walked out to check the mailbox. He came back empty-handed.

"Mary, where's the mail?" he asked.

"I don't know."

"Do you think it hasn't come yet?" he pressed, his tone gentle but insistent.

"I think I picked it up."

"Then where is it?" His voice had an edge of concern.

"I don't know!" The words came out sharper than I intended.

"You have to try hard, Mary," he said, "to make your memory work, because it's really important. Pushing your brain to remember things will help you. Like, you need to always put the mail in the tray on my desk. Think. Where'd you put it today?"

"I thought I put it in your tray." I said.

"It's not there, Mary. You can't lose the mail. I need it."

We searched all over the house. But it was nowhere to be found.

THE NEXT DAY, as I thought about Mary's TBI, I sank onto the living room couch and picked up a magazine from the coffee table. When I flipped through it, three envelopes fell into my lap. The missing mail.

I stared at it for a moment, a sense of relief filling me. Two of the envelopes were bills. I called out to Mary, and within moments, I heard to the tap-tap of her shoes on the hardwood floor as she headed toward me. When I showed her the envelopes, she stared with a blank look. No recognition. No memory of yesterday's lost mail.

"You have to keep trying, Mary. It's very important you remember." I looked at her intently but didn't mention the bills.

"I'll try, Tom."

I heard the uncertainty in her voice, despite the positive reply, and knew I'd have to keep reminding her. Maybe the postman had accidentally placed the mail inside the magazine, but either way, Mary needed to keep improving her memory. I recalled memories of her before the accident— her can-do attitude, and enthusiasm—and I knew she'd want me to keep pressing, to ask for more, to hold her accountable. It was the only way forward.

"Okay, good," I said. "You've got to keep trying to remember. It's really important."

"I can do it," she replied, her voice tinged with determination.

In that moment, I glimpsed the strong woman I'd married.

DYLAN AND CODY remained distant. They couldn't reconcile the mother I'd once been with who I was now. The disconnection between us was a chasm I didn't know how to build a bridge across.

The day of Cody's wedding arrived, and although I couldn't ignore the distance between us, my heart swelled with joy for him and Beth. My memories of her were faint, but I was thrilled to have another daughter in the family.

The ceremony was held at a venue Cody and Beth had selected. The decorations were beautiful, with gorgeous arrangements of pink and white roses, their delicate fragrance floating through the room.

As the reception began, a slow song filled the air. Tom reached out his hand. "Dance with me?"

He led me to the dance floor, and as he pulled me close, the world around us melted away. For a moment, it almost felt like it was our own wedding.

"Are you happy?" he asked, smiling at me.

There was still so much unknown to me, but in that moment, as I looked at Cody and saw his face beaming, my heart filled with peace.

I nodded. "I am, Tom. This is wonderful."

He pulled me close again, and we continued to dance. When the music ended and we stopped, I felt a twinge of disappointment. But the day had been long, the excitement taking its toll. Tom and I spent the rest of the reception resting and people-watching.

When the reception ended, we hugged Cody and Beth, offering our well wishes and love. We followed them outside, where congratulations echoed all around, and waved while they climbed into the white stretch limo Tom had rented. Their faces glowed with the kind of happiness only newlyweds have.

The limo began to roll, and the newlyweds popped their heads through the sunroof, grinning and waving at everyone. We waved again as happy goodbyes rang out from the crowd. As the limo picked up speed, Cody put his arm around Beth, and they lowered themselves back inside. When the limo disappeared around a bend, they were gone.

Feeling both happy and sad, I brushed a tear from my cheek.

Tom pulled me into his arms, pressing me close. "The ceremony was great," he murmured.

The wedding was a bright, uplifting moment, and I wanted to hold on to the memories.

35

Betrayal

As I ate breakfast, I gazed out the window at the new day and let my mind wander. Then a name broke through the fog—*Paula. I remember her. She lives nearby.*

I set down my mug and found Tom in the kitchen cleaning up.

"I remembered someone," I said. "Paula. I'm going to call her."

He turned to me with a quiet look, and said, "She hasn't spoken with you since the accident."

He was always happy when another memory surfaced, but something about his reply this time was different.

"Oh?"

"Yes, and I wouldn't expect too much," he said.

Undeterred, I made the call.

"Hello?" Paula said.

"Hi, it's Mary."

There was a silence on the other end. "Hey," she said at last. "What's up?"

The ability to make small talk was one of the things I'd lost, so I jumped right in. "My brain injury has caused me to forget some things, so can I ask you a few questions?"

I'd barely spoken the words when Paula lashed out, "Your brain injury is too hard for me! I can't help you!"

Taken aback, I asked, "Why not?"

"It's too hard for me!"

My mind raced. Too hard for *her*? I had a brain injury and was trying to piece together answers, and her statement was absurd.

Suddenly, memories flooded me—Paula repeatedly calling me and asking for advice, her gossiping about others, always wanting attention, and lamenting her fading relationship with her husband. I'd spent a lot of time helping her.

Anger rushed through me. I already had too many problems and couldn't take on Paula's.

"I don't know why I didn't see it before," I whispered, more to myself than her.

"What'd you say?" she demanded.

"I can't believe you!" I yelled. "Don't ever talk to me again!"

I slammed down the phone, the sound echoing through the living room.

Tom crossed the room in seconds, concern on his face.

"Are you all right?"

I told him what Paula had said.

"I'm through with her. If she ever calls here again, tell her I said so. I don't want anything to do with her anymore. Ever."

Tom gently touched my arm. "Maybe if you call your brother Joe, he can talk with you."

I nodded. I wanted to call someone who loved me despite my injury. I needed people in my life who accepted me for who I was.

I picked up the phone and called Joe.

"You won't believe what someone just said to me," I blurted the second he answered the phone.

"What?"

I told him everything about the call.

He was quiet for a moment, then sighed. "Mary, you know you don't need anybody like that."

"I'm trying to remember—" I started.

"Well, you should."

As he spoke, more memories returned. "I was a good friend to her," I said, remembering I'd given her a lot of help.

"She's not a friend," Joe said with conviction. "I'm sorry she did that. You know you can always call me. Anytime."

He was right. Paula wasn't a friend, not even before the accident. I just hadn't seen it. Her words—"too hard for me"— echoed through my mind in disbelief. I was dealing with the blackness of brain injury, and Paula's behavior, shocking and painful, was a betrayal.

But the memories that had returned were helpful. Pieces of my past. They were mine. And I was slowly finding my way back. One piece at a time.

Lord, thank you for my memories.

36

Six Flags

One Month Before the Accident

The long-awaited Saturday had finally arrived, and when Dylan and Cody showed up at our house, we all piled into my car. Mary and I were taking the boys to Six Flags over Georgia, an amusement park just outside of Austell, an hour from our home. It was our family ritual to go there every summer, and everyone loved it. As I pulled out of the driveway, the car filled with laughter and the kind of lively banter only families could have.

After we made our way past the ticket booths and into the park, the boys took the lead. In each line, we waited eagerly. Heartbeats quickening. Excitement growing. The roller coasters were Mary's favorite. I wouldn't go on them— they were too crazy for me. But she couldn't resist laughing, screaming, and twisting through every turn with the boys. We wandered through the park, watched entertaining shows, and laughed along with the crowds.

The shows were a good break from the heat of the day and the busy rides, and gave Mary and me a chance to rest. And we grabbed snacks at the concession stand. Popcorn for us. Cotton candy for Dylan and Cody.

"Isn't this fun?" Mary asked me, as we waited for a new show to begin.

"It's great. The perfect break from our jobs. Thank you for everything you did to make this such a good trip for all of us."

"You know I'm happy to do it. Besides, if you share a little more of that popcorn, we can call it even." She winked playfully as the lights began to dim before the next show started.

After a pizza lunch, the boys were chomping at the bit to get away and see the park on their own.

Mary told them, "Dad and I will meet you guys at the car at 5:00. Don't be late."

When it was time to leave the park, Mary and I lingered over each step toward the car, savoring the satisfaction of a day well spent. Back at home, we gave the boys warm hugs and told them we loved them, and they promised to come visit the next weekend. They had moved out of our house only recently, and we were still adjusting to the empty nest.

As Mary and I sat on the back porch, the evening sun covered the lake in liquid gold.

"What a wonderful day we had," she murmured. "Next year, we need to ride the Scorch—"

"Don't even say it!" I laughed.

"What?" she asked, her lips curving into that irresistible, playful pout.

"You know what. I can't take those roller coasters."

And there it was. Her beautiful laugh.

"I'm glad you had a good time today," I said.

Now, as I reflected on that family trip to Six Flags, I wondered why God had allowed the TBI to happen to the sweetest, kindest person in the world.

37

The Blessing and the Curse

One Year After

"Why did this injury have to happen?" I asked Tom again.

"We're not in control of everything," he said. "The accident wasn't your fault. It just happened."

"I hate that it did!" I buried my face in my hands.

"Mary, you still have a life. And I love you. You need to let go of your anger. If you don't, it'll cause more problems."

Easy for him to say. But even as I thought it, I felt guilty. The injury had upended his life too.

Lord, how did this injury steal my memory?

My brain kept recycling frustration and anger. After repeatedly discussing it with Tom and my counselor, I decided to try listening more to my thoughts and feelings about things before acting angry.

A Bible verse I'd learned as a child popped into my mind: "Your word is a lamp for my feet, a light on my path."[4] The words of the verse and the fact I'd remembered it lightened my frustration.

As time passed, I realized being angry wasn't helping, and my temper cooled some more. But I remained quick to get upset without warning. Tom took the heat and encouraged me to be calm. I found being calmer allowed me to think better, and I wanted even more to stop being angry. I thought about Tom's love and how thankful I was for my relationship with him, and I felt a little better.

WALKING INTO THE living room, I found Mary in her recliner, listening to rock music on the TV.

"Hey, darling. What are you doing?"

"Listening."

I smiled. Music had always been a big part of her life. "Do you remember singing solos in church?"

"A little. But music sounds different now."

"In what way?"

"I hear the four different parts of a song—the soprano, alto, tenor, and bass."

I listened to the song, but it sounded like it always had.

"Before the injury," she continued, "I could only hear the notes for my soprano part. But now, I hear the notes for all the parts."

"What?"

---

4 Psalm 119:105

"I hear music differently. I hear each part individually, separate from the other parts."

Mary was unfazed by her new ability, but it struck me as a breakthrough of sorts. She comprehended music in a whole new way.

I had come to accept that this was how it was with her injury—living with the unusual.

ONE MORNING, TOM said quietly, "Mary, we need to sell our house and move to a smaller one. Somewhere I can take care of you better."

"What?" I asked in surprise.

"You're more important than this big house and the yard. And I can't take care of you and everything here and still give you what you need."

"So you want to move?"

He nodded. "Darling, I'm trying to help us. This house isn't working."

"You don't know what it's like to wake up every day and not—"

"Mary, this isn't sustainable."

Silence stretched between us. Finally I said, "Where would we go?" It was the first thing my brain latched onto.

He stepped closer. "We'll find a place that works better. Something you'll like."

I swallowed hard. "Okay."

"Mary, we really need this." He gave me a hug. "I'll be with you every step of the way."

We prayed about moving and put it in God's hands.

The idea of moving scared me. I asked Tom lots of questions about it. His answers stirred faint memories and brought new questions. Determination settled over me: since he wanted us to move, I did too.

Needing to move was a blessing and a curse. The blessing was distraction—it focused my thinking away from the injury. The curse was the added stress, which pressed heavily on me.

My head injury was still new and daunting. Just getting through each day took everything I had. I tried to keep thinking about the move, but exhaustion took over. My brain couldn't keep going.

THE COMPLICATIONS OF Mary's TBI kept pushing both of us past the limits of our patience. I worried about her ability to help with the move and knew I'd have to stay close to her. I tried to explain things in new ways, but her cognition was very disrupted and her thoughts jumped around. There was no pattern to her difficulties except confusion and inconsistency. She could have a good day, like at Cody's wedding, but it didn't last long.

Flashes of memory were becoming more common, but they still didn't stay with her. One minute she'd remember something; the next, it was gone. She'd start telling me something, only to lose her train of thought and trail off, hunting for words that wouldn't come. I never knew what she would say or do next. She wanted to talk about whatever popped into her head, but her struggle to express herself—and to understand me—made those conversations hard.

I found myself wondering about her progress. Why is she so confused? Why hasn't more of her understanding returned? Why do memories that return keep slipping away? Yet occasionally, she'd remember something that stayed with her, or she'd complete a task with less difficulty, and I knew she was improving.

Through it all, her determination to cope never faded, and her effort reminded me of the love and admiration I had always felt for her.

TOM AND I BEGAN taking drives to look for a new house. One afternoon, a song came on the radio that I recognized—and before I knew it, I was singing along.

Tom glanced at me with a grin. "Do you remember we met because you sang a song?"

"Sort of," I said.

"And now, I still love hearing you sing."

"Since I can hear all the different parts of a song, I can sing your tenor part, and you can sing along with me." I chuckled.

He gave me a quick look. "Do you always hear all the parts now?"

"Always."

Singing was a way I could make Tom happy, and that made me happy too. I decided to sing more often.

Suddenly, another memory flared—my summers touring with the Billy Graham Crusade.

When I was fifteen, my parents belonged to a church in Oklahoma City, and our family was there so often it felt like a second home. I sang in the youth choir, and that spring the director announced we would attend a Billy Graham Crusade at another church. The director asked me to sing a solo there, as I often did during our services.

At the Crusade, I stepped onto the stage with the choir behind me, and I sang with them as my backup. After the applause, we were led off stage into a small side room. A man walked in with my director and they came straight to me. He told me he'd enjoyed my solo and invited me to tour with the Billy Graham Crusade that summer. My parents agreed it was a good opportunity.

When summer came, I traveled from city to city across Oklahoma with the Crusade. It was exhilarating. The next summer I did it again, in Texas. After that, cosmetology school pulled me in a different direction, so I wasn't able to tour with the Crusade again.

Filled with happiness, I turned my thoughts back to our search for a new home.

DURING ANOTHER HOUSE-HUNTING drive, Tom and I found a smaller house we wanted to buy. On the way home, we discussed our plans—a major part was selling our current house first.

Arriving home, we found a letter tucked into the handle of the front door. Someone had driven past our house, and they wanted to buy it. It felt like an answered prayer and things fell into place with ease. A few weeks later, we sold our house and bought the new one. The person who bought our old house let us rent it back from them for a month, while we moved out.

I faced many questions about moving. Some needed to be answered quickly, causing me to push myself to think faster.

TOM TOLD ME to evaluate everything in our house and decide what to keep. The task felt enormous. As I helped him sort through our belongings, selecting what to keep and what to get rid of, I tried to sort my thoughts and do the same.

I lifted a snow globe to the light and studied it. I didn't remember where it came from, and it held no meaning for me. Its value was in the memory, and the memory was gone.

I shook the globe and watched its tiny blizzard swirl. Each shake caused a different storm—no two alike. And suddenly, I saw myself in it. Shaking a snow globe turned a peaceful scene into a storm, and a brain injury did the same to a person's thoughts. And like the snowflakes, a survivor's thoughts settled into new patterns.

I wrapped the globe in bubble wrap and tucked it safely into a moving box, feeling protective of its fragile weather.

THE KITCHEN WAS half-packed, boxes scattered across the hardwood floor. I turned a faded coffee mug in my hands— the one Tom liked.

He stood at the counter, carefully wrapping glasses in moving paper.

"You still want this?" I asked.

He glanced over his shoulder and smiled. "Yes."

I nodded slowly. "You'll never toss it."

"Nope," he grinned. "You don't like how it looks?"

"I don't remember where we got it, and it's faded," I said.

He stopped packing and turned to me. "You don't have to remember everything, Mary."

"But I want to. I want to remember who I was—who we were."

He sat at the table with me, resting his arms on it. "You're still you. And we're still us."

I looked down at the mug, then set it aside and reached for his hand. "I remember the night we danced in the kitchen. When you burned the chicken."

He laughed. I loved the sound of it.

"That night," I said softly, "everything felt so easy."

"It wasn't all easy," he said. "We just believed things could be good. And that's what made the difference."

"I want to believe again."

AT OUR NEW house, I tried to settle in, but my memory was still a challenge.

I stood barefoot in the new kitchen, unsure where the coffee filters had ended up. I opened a cabinet—wrong one—then another. Still wrong.

Tom stepped into the room, and when he saw me, his face brightened. "Need help?"

"I can't find the filters," I said. "They're somewhere around here."

He smiled and walked over to one of the boxes near the fridge. Without saying anything, he pulled it open, rummaged through it, and pulled out the filters. Then, with a flourish, he held up the faded blue mug.

"I'll need this too," he said, setting it on the counter.

I stared at it for a moment. "You want to use that?"

"Of course I do. You know I love it."

Giving him a slow smile, I said, "I still think it's worn out."

"Just because something is faded or worn, doesn't mean it's not still valuable."

He nudged it toward me.

I picked up the mug. It felt familiar in my hands, and I sighed, realizing it was important to Tom. A comfort rose inside me, knowing he still thought I was valuable too, even with my injury.

We set up the coffee maker together and started it brewing, and while we waited for it to finish, we unwrapped a couple more boxes.

As Tom poured our coffee, I leaned against the counter. "It doesn't feel like home yet," I said.

He nodded. "But it will."

He handed me my cup. Our fingers touched briefly. No fireworks, no drama. Just a quiet moment, simple and shared.

THE CLOSET IN the new bedroom was filled with boxes that Tom had stacked, and nothing was where it should be.

I stood in the doorway, trying to figure out how to find what I wanted. I'd come in to get a sweater, but now I couldn't remember which one.

I felt it creeping in—the fog. That lost feeling. My hands moved through the boxes, my heart pounding for no reason I could understand.

"Come on," I whispered to myself. "Just pick one."

But I couldn't. And I didn't know why. I couldn't even remember what color I had wanted. I backed away, clutching a scarf instead.

Tom walked in behind me, pausing when he saw my face. "Hey," he said gently. "You all right?"

My voice was thin, shaky. "I don't know what I'm doing. I can't even pick a stupid sweater. I came in here to do one thing, and I can't—"

"Hey. Hey. It's okay." He reached for me.

"No, it's *not* okay. I'm still forgetting things. And I don't feel like myself in this house. I barely feel comfortable *anywhere*."

"Honey, you're getting better. You don't have to feel like you yet. That'll come. But until it does, I'm here, and I'll help you. And we'll just do things one step, one box, at a time."

I swallowed. "What if I never find myself again?"

He looked at me gently. "Then we'll build someone new. Together."

THE HOUSE WAS quiet. Tom had gone to the grocery, and I was alone.

I moved slowly through the rooms, past boxes we still hadn't touched—"Office," "Books," "Pictures." We'd unpacked the essentials, but the rest remained like unopened memories, waiting to be revealed.

In the kitchen, an empty shelf caught my eye. I wandered back to the unpacked boxes and opened the one marked "Pictures." With surprising speed, my hands sorted through the contents until I found it: a photo of our younger selves—Tom grinning, my hair wind-blown. I hardly recognized myself, but something about the picture pulled at me. I smiled, carrying it to the shelf.

Next, I opened the cabinet where I'd put the coffee mugs and picked up the faded blue one. I took it to the shelf and placed it there. One photo. One coffee mug. They didn't match, but they belonged there, in that small space I was claiming—not because it made me feel whole, but because it reminded me that I didn't have to be.

I stood back, looking at the two items—special, unique, faded. Like me.

TOM CAME HOME a little later with the groceries.

We unpacked in comfortable silence. Then he noticed the kitchen shelf and paused. His gaze lingered, taking it in.

"You did that?" he asked quietly.

I nodded.

"You put *that* mug out?"

"It earned its place," I said.

He turned toward me, a smile in his eyes. "It's good."

"It's a start," I replied.

We stood there for a moment, side by side, looking at two small items that were faded and worn, but belonged. And even though things weren't fully right—not my memory, not our past—we both knew that we were still building something. And we were building it together.

OUR NEW NEIGHBORHOOD had sidewalks, and we took a walk every day. Tom held my hand as we went, and we talked about everything. Gradually, I grew stronger, and we started walking farther, exploring side streets, and saying hello to neighbors. With each walk, I felt more connected to Tom and the world around me, and I gained more confidence.

I'm doing it. Making a new life.

The injury was still a giant obstacle, but a new sense of happiness and pride was growing inside me.

38

The Dental Office Visit

A Year and a Half After

Tom made an appointment for us to have our teeth cleaned at the office where I had worked for twelve years. The idea of going to the dentist puzzled me.

"I brush my teeth, Tom, every morning and night. So why do I need to go to an office where they do what I already do?"

"Just to make sure everything's good," he said.

I shrugged, though I couldn't help but feel a little curious. After all, it was the place I had worked.

"It's different," Tom said. "You'll see. You wouldn't have worked there if you didn't believe it was important." He gave me a reassuring pat on the back. "Maybe you'll remember something," he added as we climbed into the car.

After a short drive, we pulled into a parking lot, and a red brick building stood before us. It had white-trimmed windows and a white front door.

"This used to be a house," Tom said. "Dr. Smith remodeled it into a dental office before you started working here, and your patients always said it felt comforting. Does it look familiar?"

I hesitated, then nodded. "Yes. And no."

He turned off the engine and smiled. "Come on. Let's go in."

Something in his voice made me wonder if this moment was about more than just getting our teeth cleaned.

Walking up the sidewalk, I thought about how many times I must have done it before, but my mind had no answer.

Tom opened the door, and we stepped inside.

The warmth of the office struck me, and I paused for a moment, taking it all in. The waiting room had two couches on either side of a coffee table covered with magazines. Four armchairs were positioned near a fireplace, which, though unlit, created a sense of cozy welcome.

"Do you remember this?" Tom's voice pulled me back to the present.

"It feels like I've been here before," I said, my voice hesitant.

A woman in yellow scrubs spotted us from across the room, and a big smile crossed her face. She hurried over, her eyes lighting up. "Mary! Oh, it's so good to see you!" She pulled me into a tight hug, her enthusiasm both overwhelming and oddly reassuring.

Other people quickly joined her, their greetings warm and heartfelt. "We've missed you so much," one of them said. Their smiles were genuine, and the affection they offered wrapped around me like a familiar embrace. But I couldn't shake the feeling of watching a reunion that was familiar yet foreign. I smiled hesitantly, trying to mirror their warmth.

Some of the faces seemed familiar, and the feeling of memories tugged at me. "Thank you," I murmured, unsure what else to say.

Tom squeezed my hand. "Let's sit down."

As we waited, I glanced around, my eyes catching on the shelves behind the reception desk, holding red and blue folders. A memory seemed to hoover just out of reach. I could almost see myself pulling a folder out, looking through its pages. The sensation was vivid, but I couldn't connect it to anything specific.

"The wall of patient folders," I whispered. "I remember that."

Tom followed my gaze. "You used those folders. You were proud of the work you did."

A sense of memory pressed at me vaguely. "I wish I remembered more," I said. It was frustrating to feel myself on the brink of a memory, only to fall short time and time again.

Tom didn't say anything, just gave my hand another squeeze. When it was time for his cleaning, I went into the operatory with him. *Operatory.* Had someone mentioned that word, or was it something I remembered?

As I sat in a room where I'd apparently spent countless hours, the sights, sounds, and smells slowly began to feel achingly familiar. The look of the room, the faint metallic clink of the instruments, the hum of the suction tool, the scent of disinfectant.

I closed my eyes, and a flash of memory returned: the rhythm of handing instruments to the doctor, the confidence in my movements, the satisfaction of my job. *I'd been good at this—hadn't I?*

Later, as we left the office, I felt a new mix of emotions. The warmth of familiarity, the ache of what I'd lost, and gratitude for what I had. Tom took my hand as we walked to the car, and I drew strength from his support.

"You were happy here," he said. "You loved your job and the people. You were always smiling."

I glanced back at the building one last time. "I wish I could remember that."

"It's okay if you don't," he said.

I nodded, feeling the truth of his words settle over me. Life was different now, but maybe that was okay.

I COULDN'T STOP asking Tom questions—about how to talk with people, about events around me, and about anything else that came to mind. He answered and guided the conversation gently onto new topics.

Gradually, I could follow the ebb and flow of conversation more easily. My ability was still inconsistent, but as it improved, the fog in my mind lifted a little more.

My ability to recall a memory was also improving, yet still, it felt like trying to grab water. I learned that saving a new memory worked much better than recalling an old one. Trying to summon an old memory was so difficult that often, I just couldn't do it.

I began to feel a new sense of progress, and I enjoyed the feeling. The more I recovered, the more I wanted to get my life back to normal. Then the irony hit me: I didn't know what normal was, so I had to keep searching for answers.

AS MARY KEPT struggling to handle everyday activities, her cognitive ability was slowly improving, but her reactions to various situations continued to fluctuate widely. Her thoughts were constantly in flux—shifting and inconsistent.

Her aphasia had improved, but she still battled with communication. She strained to understand what people said to her, and to speak without confusing others. The subtle nuances of conversation were especially hard for her.

Prior to the accident, she'd been a quick thinker, highly intuitive, and adept in conversation. I reminded her that beneath the surface of conversation, there were multiple layers of unspoken communication. It surprised her, and she pressed me with questions.

"Mary, there are undercurrents in people's speech, like their feelings and attitude, separate from just the words they say. If you pay attention to those messages, it'll help you."

I assured her the subtleties were a normal part of communication, and she just needed to relearn them, but mostly, they remained beyond her understanding. Abstract concepts were especially hard for her; she did best with concrete facts.

Every day, she pushed herself to understand—determined and relentless, as if sheer willpower could restore her mind. The harder she pushed, the more her thoughts shifted.

Her thinking now functioned in a completely different way from before the accident. She saw everything through a mix of both her old and new thinking, in ways that made her unpredictable. Her thoughts often changed direction like the wind, without warning. I never knew what she might say or do. But I didn't spend time trying to figure it all out. I didn't need to. I loved her, and that was what I held on to.

As time passed, her thoughts kept evolving, pulling us both deeper into unknown territory. I couldn't predict where her TBI would take us.

I GRADUALLY FOUND myself paying more attention to the unspoken messages in conversation—the speaker's tone, the pauses, the hints beneath the words. Still, none of it came easily. People's motives and intentions were even harder to grasp. The more I interacted with others, the more I struggled to decipher what was truly being communicated.

I became aware there were gray areas in conversation, and it puzzled me. I realized there was sometimes a difference between what people said and what was true. I asked Tom to help me understand how others thought, and how their thinking differed from mine.

"Everyone thinks differently," he said. "You just need to figure out your own."

When I asked what others thought about my head injury, he gave me a steady look.

"People without a TBI can't understand what it's like to have one. Especially a severe one. It's like trying to describe what colors look like to someone who can't see. And you can't expect them to understand."

From experience, I knew that trying to explain my injury was too complicated, and some people just walked away. But I didn't have that option; the injury was part of me, whether I liked it or not. I had to learn to live with it the best way I could.

"Let me read you a Bible verse you've heard before," Tom said. "Do not be anxious about anything, but in every situation, by prayer and petition, with thanksgiving, present your requests to God."[5]

"I remember that."

"Good. I hoped you would. I think you should keep praying and asking God for answers."

As I considered what Tom said, I kept thinking about how people spoke and acted. Some people didn't seem to care much about others, and the idea unsettled me.

"Tom, how can people expect others to be there for them when they won't do the same?"

"Well, that's just how some people are, Mary. Here, let me pray for us." He took my hands. "Lord, thank you for being our Lord. Help us understand the things you want us to. We pray for people to care about others, and we pray for those who don't have a relationship with you. Thank you for loving us, and help us do your will. Amen."

---

[5] Philippians 4:6

I thought about Tom and how he still loved me despite my injury, and a sudden realization hit: *I don't want to worry about what others think of me. Tom loves me, and I love him. That's what matters.*

He looked at me and smiled.

Memories of who I'd been before the accident were still murky, but with Tom's love, I would do whatever it took to rebuild my life—our life.

I smiled back. "I love you."

39

Weaving a Workable Net

Almost Two Years After

We had reached a turning point in Mary's recovery. Now, while inconsistencies in her cognition continued to dominate, her good days were becoming more common.

Each time she recalled a memory, conquered a challenge, or achieved something new, I saw the joy and pride in her eyes. It was inspiring and lifted both of us. I encouraged her to embrace the new version of herself that she was becoming, and as she did, her confidence kept growing.

I continued sharing stories from our past and reminding her of all the reasons she meant so much to me, and brighter smiles spread across her face. Seeing those smiles again filled me with happiness. It reminded me of the Mary of my past. After the accident, she had changed in ways that people unfamiliar with TBI couldn't imagine, but as she kept healing and growing, my admiration for her was deepening. I cherished not just the woman she was becoming, but the new relationship we were building.

SITTING ON THE edge of our bed, surrounded by the quiet of the room, I reached over to the nightstand and picked up a photograph. Mary's smile, radiant, just as it had always been before everything changed, lit up the picture. I couldn't help but smile back. That smile, her laugh—the sound that could brighten even the dark days—I missed it more than words could express.

As Mary faced each day, her mind tried to weave a workable net of general understanding. She never gave up, even though her memory was faulty, her thoughts wavered constantly, and comprehension came in only short bursts.

It was hard to watch her struggle with conversation—like placing an order with a waitress or talking to a doctor's receptionist. Some days, those conversations were riddled with miscommunication; other days, they were smoother. When it was smoother, it was like catching a fleeting glimpse of the person she had been—before the fog. Yet through it all, she kept trying.

Lord, I don't know how to do this without you. Show me how to be the husband Mary needs.

"Tom," Mary called from the other room.

The sound of her voice was still music to my ears. Even now, after the TBI, it stirred something inside me. She was the love of my life, and even as she fought through the shadows of her injury, she owned my heart.

I missed who we used be—how we navigated life together, how her laughter once filled the space between us with joy. I missed our quiet moments of unspoken understanding. But I still loved her—completely. Nothing, not even the TBI, could change that. I would keep taking care of her, no matter what it took. I'd be her strength when she couldn't find her own, and gently remind her of who she had been—and who she still was—despite the injury.

I held the photograph a moment longer—enjoying her smile, captured forever, untouched by pain or confusion. Slowly, I set it back on the nightstand, drew a deep breath, and went to find her.

NEARLY EVERY DAY, I sat in my recliner reflecting on what was important to me.

I thought about how a brain injury changes a person's thinking. I knew I could try to explain the injury to someone endlessly, and the truth of it would remain out of reach. It was just too complex.

As I tapped my foot to the music, a nagging guilt tugged at me. Tom had given up a career he loved—a life he'd built for himself—to care for me full-time. It didn't seem fair. He said he had no regret, and I believed him, but I felt bad that his life had been upended along with mine.

I couldn't remember the woman I had been before the accident, but I knew I wasn't like her. I asked Tom to tell me about her again.

"You worked at a job you loved," he said. "You cooked, did the laundry, and enjoyed gardening with me. You were a great mom. You loved church and singing. You did so much, and you did it all very well."

The woman he described felt like a stranger. I couldn't imagine doing those things now. Tom handled the household chores—the grocery shopping, cooking, cleaning, and laundry. He did it all. And somehow, he also still asked me out on dates. He'd look at me with a hopeful expression, waiting for my answer, and when I said yes, as always, he'd tell me what time to be ready.

I loved the anticipation of our dates—getting dressed nicely, doing my hair, spraying on perfume. The excitement made my heart flutter. Tom enjoyed taking me out, holding my hand, and opening doors for me. And the way he looked at me, with endless admiration, telling me how beautiful I was, how much he loved me ... it made me wonder again about the woman I had been, and the relationship we had before.

Our dates and neighborhood walks helped improve my social skills and balance, each step a small victory. Tom began taking me into new situations more often, reminding me I needed to keep practicing. Still, the hurdles persisted—my memory struggled, my words faltered, and I kept falling. Tom took me back to my orthopedist.

The doctor x-rayed my knees, then told me that my falling had damaged my second knee so badly that I needed another total knee replacement.

Tom tried to comfort me, but I cried on the way home.

"Sweetheart, we can do this," he said.

I wanted to believe him, but the thought of another knee replacement was crushing. His hand held mine, steady and sure, a quiet promise he'd face it with me.

He reminded me the Bible says: "Trust in the Lord with all your heart."[6]

"Mary, let's keep giving everything to God and try not to worry too much."

"I'm trying," I whispered, wiping at my tears. I clung to hope that things would get better.

Lord, I can't do this without you.

THE TIME HAD come for Dylan to finish school and visit us, but Mary and I hadn't heard from him in weeks—his phone calls had stopped, leaving a growing silence between us. We looked forward to seeing him, and having him at our house for a couple of weeks would be good for Mary.

I waited a little longer, but when he still hadn't called, I took matters into my own hands.

When Dylan answered the phone, I got right to the point.

"Have you finished school and returned to Atlanta?"

There was a long pause. "Yes," he said, his voice distant.

"So, when are you coming to visit?" I asked.

He hesitated again. "Uh, I'm not."

"What? You said you'd visit after school."

"Sorry, Dad. I'm not coming."

"Dylan, Mom's been waiting a long time to see you."

---

[6] Proverbs 3:5

"I know, but I can't see ... I've changed my mind."
He sighed.

"That's not right. And you didn't think you should tell us?"
Silence.

"Dylan, you know Mom's going to be hurt?"

"I'm sorry."

I was trying to understand. He had promised he would come. It never occurred to me he wouldn't. "Why are you backing out?"

"Because I want to hang out with my friends before I have to get a job," he blurted.

"I'm sorry to hear that."

"Yeah, Dad ..." he said, quieter now. "I just can't."

Our relationship with Dylan was already strained, but hearing him now, it was clear he was struggling more than we had known.

"I'll tell Mom," I said. "There's nothing else to say."

I hung up, knowing disappointment would hit Mary hard. We had been looking forward to a good visit.

Lord, we put our relationship with the two younger boys in your hands. Help them restore their relationship with us.

I STARED AT Tom as I listened to his side of the call.

"Isn't he coming?" I asked when he hung up.

"He said he can't make it," Tom replied.

My heart sank. I couldn't believe Dylan wasn't coming. We had given him much of our limited time and energy, at a time when I badly needed help myself. I had so looked forward to our time together, but now that hope was gone.

I was unable to stop the tears sliding down my face. My fingers absently smoothed the pillow in my lap.

It wasn't just Dylan—it was Cody too. Inconceivable as it was, both of them had turned away. Tom and I had always done our best to be loving parents, provide for them, and teach them the values we believed in. We had given them a good loving family, and yet, in my time of need, they had become distant.

I thought about Leo and was thankful for the good relationship he still had with us. He continued to care, reach out, and be supportive. I hoped that even if Dylan and Cody didn't want to stay connected with us, that they would with Leo.

I shared my feelings with Tom.

"Darling, you didn't do anything wrong. Dylan's an adult, and he's making his own decisions."

"I don't understand him. Why won't he come?" I asked.

"I don't know," Tom said, shaking his head. "I know you feel discouraged but try not to be. Hopefully he'll come around." He wrapped his arms around me and held me close.

I drew comfort from his embrace, and I prayed that God would watch over all my children.

40

Tug-of-War

Two Years After

"Tom," I said, "my thoughts always keep wandering."

"You're getting better," he said gently. "And it's normal for thoughts to wander sometimes."

When anyone spoke, my attention often drifted—their words fading into the background as I thought of other things. Sometimes I could return to listening to the speaker, but other times, I had to interrupt, asking them to repeat what they'd just said. It was exasperating.

As I tried to focus my attention on things happening around me, like when people spoke, it felt like my mind was playing tug-of-war, trying to prove that it was in charge, not me.

When Tom noticed I had drifted from a conversation, he'd gently guide my attention back. No matter the challenge, his answer was always the same: "We can do this." His belief in me helped me believe in myself.

"Your faith in me gives me hope," I told him one day after he'd gently redirected my attention for the second time. I smiled.

"Look at that smile," he said, eyes full of warmth. "You need to quit worrying so much and start enjoying yourself more."

His love inspired me to be the best wife I could be. I rose from the table, slipped my arms around him, and kissed his cheek. "I love you," I whispered.

He turned and kissed me, and in that moment, my feelings for him soared.

Then he asked gently, "Do you want to try going back to church?"

"No." I hated turning him down, but I was still often overwhelmed by confusion and didn't feel ready to try church again.

I crossed the room. "I'm going to let the dog out," I said, opening the back door.

A puzzled look crossed Tom's face. "Darling, we don't have a dog. We have a cat. Dolly. Remember?"

Just like that, after a perfect moment with Tom, I sank back into frustration.

Why did I call Dolly a dog?

I sat down and closed my eyes, willing my thoughts to clear up.

Tom came over and pulled me into his arms. "Hey, don't worry about it. Even with mistakes, you're doing great." He held me close. "I love you, darling," he said, and the warmth of his love calmed the storm in my mind.

TOM CONTINUED TAKING me out on various dates. Sometimes they felt like an adventure—new, exciting, and fun. Even though I couldn't remember every detail of our dates, I loved how it felt to be with him.

One day, he took me to a street lined with a cheering crowd, where runners were racing past. As we stood along the street edge, Tom handed me two cups of water. "For the runners!" he said, his smile contagious.

The crowd was full of energy, shouting and cheering. The slap of footsteps on the pavement, the rush of movement, the calls of encouragement—it was thrilling. We joined in, handing out water to the runners as they passed. My heart raced along with them, even though I didn't know much about the race.

As we stood there, I caught a glimpse of Tom's face—grinning, watching me with a look that made me feel good. It was in small moments like that, just being together, that I felt connected again, even with my memories still clouded.

Gradually, my life was coming back together, piece by piece. It wasn't fast, but it was happening. And I had finally stopped fainting, another step of progress.

Even with my weak memory, I knew one thing for sure—I was falling for Tom, and that was a memory I didn't want to lose.

I WOULD OFTEN begin an activity, only to forget what I'd started to do. As I struggled in those moments, anxiety crept in.

Lord, please keep me safe and help me remember things.

Other times, I finished what I started, and it felt good.

Through it all, the only pattern to living with the brain injury was that there was no pattern.

Still, I could tell my memory was improving.

One morning, as Tom and I were having coffee, he picked up the Bible and said, "I want us to read the book of Proverbs each day during our coffee time."

"Oh?" I set my cup down.

"Yes. We should read one chapter a day, and talk about it as we go."

"That sounds good."

He opened the Bible. "We'll start this morning."

The proverbs were interesting, and we enjoyed discussing them. One day he read this verse to me: "Commit to the Lord whatever you do, and he will establish your plans."[7]

Tom read it again, then smiled at me. "I've committed my plan for you to keep healing to the Lord, so I know you'll keep getting better."

---

[7] Proverbs 16:3

41

The Fire of Necessity

After my head injury, I never drove again because I knew I couldn't—and I didn't want to. Tom and I hadn't even discussed the idea. We were both sure I never would.

But one day, everything changed.

We had dinner out one evening, and then Tom started throwing up. It went on all night, his face gray with exhaustion by morning.

"I need a doctor," he muttered.

"Okay. Where do we go?" My voice sounded steadier than I felt.

"There's a walk-in clinic a few miles away." He paused, gripping the trash can.

"How are you going to drive and hold that can in your lap?" I asked.

"I'm"—he lurched forward and threw up—"not. You have to drive."

Fear surged through me. "But Tom, I can't—"

"Mary, there's no other choice. You have to because"—he threw up again—"I can't."

Terror wrapped around my chest. The idea of getting in the driver's seat was petrifying.

"But, Tom, I'm scared—"

"Mary, you need to put that out of your mind and focus on getting me there."

"I can't!" My voice cracked. "And I don't remember how to get there!"

Between bouts of nausea, Tom said, "Call your friend Marsha. Ask her to come here"—he threw up—"and follow her to the doctor."

The thought of driving sent chills of fear through me.

"I've got the trash can. C'mon, let's go." Tom doubled over again, then walked unsteadily to the car.

Heart hammering, unable to believe what was happening, I edged into the driver's seat—my whole body trembling. I couldn't even try to start the car.

"Tom, I don't—"

He threw-up again. "I need ... you ... to do this—" Another wave of nausea hit him. "The sooner we go, the sooner it'll be over."

My hands shaking, I stabbed the key at the ignition several times before finally getting it in. Dizzy and weak, I started the engine and sat listening to it. Outside, Marsha's car pulled up, turned around, and started pulling away.

I sat frozen, gripping the wheel with both hands, unable to move.

"Tom, I'm not sure—"

"MARY. You have to—"

He bent over the trash can again, too sick to finish.

Frightened out of my mind, I stared through the windshield as Marsha's car shrank in the distance.

I took a deep breath, swallowed hard, and squeezed the wheel in a death grip. Gritting my teeth, I pressed my foot down on the brake as hard as I could. I put the car into gear. Slowly, I lifted my foot off the brake.

The car began to roll. My heart pounded wildly. I lightly pressed the gas pedal ...

I focused on Marsha's car like my life depended on it.

Gradually, I got the car up to twenty miles an hour, too frightened to go any faster.

Ahead, Marsha slowed down.

Eyes forward. Don't think. Just follow.

My mind was spinning, but my hands stayed locked in place, guiding the car.

The minutes slowly ticked by ...

I wasn't sure I could do this—but somehow, I was.

The clinic was three long miles away, down a quiet street with only one turn—no stoplights, no traffic. Somehow, we made it.

Inside, I collapsed into a chair, my body still trembling.

The doctor gave Tom a shot, and eventually, his nausea stopped. Then he drove us home.

I'd faced my fear and made it through, although unwillingly. If it hadn't been an emergency, I never would've tried to drive again. Every moment had been frightening, yet somehow, I'd done it.

Now, on the other side of that experience, I could scarcely believe it. The fear that previously felt all-consuming had lost some of its grip. It was still there, lurking in the shadows, but I felt a new sense of confidence growing.

Since I faced that, maybe I can trust myself to face more things?

I smiled, savoring the hard-won victory.

42

Laughter

Three Years After

A big thing I missed from our old life was the laughter Mary and I had always shared.

With her narrow comprehension of nuance, understanding humor wasn't easy for her, so we didn't tease or play with each other much. It was a gap in our life that I hoped would heal soon, and I began trying harder to find new ways to make her laugh. The more I worked at it, the better I got at making it happen.

One afternoon turned into an unforgettable comedy when we decided to buy a large, whole fresh fish at the grocery. Back at home, while emptying the grocery bags, I spotted a golden opportunity to make Mary laugh.

I grabbed the fish and held it up toward her face. Then, with a hand below it, I started opening and closing its bottom lip, pretending the fish was alive and talking to Mary, as I made funny comments. "Hey baby. Give me a kiss. I love you."

She shrieked in laughter, and it egged me on. The fish began "swimming" in the air, back and forth toward Mary's face, as it kept making funny comments. She leaned away laughing hysterically, and the fish swam toward her again. She took off running out of the kitchen, and with both of us laughing uncontrollably, I chased her around the house with the fish calling out to her as we ran.

Breathless from laughing so hard, we had to stop to catch our breath. Our eyes locked onto each other's and we burst out laughing again.

Mary's sense of humor was recovering more slowly than many other aspects of her personality, but in moments like this, it clicked right into place. Her laughter was a balm to my spirit, and I pursued every opportunity to make it happen.

Positive changes were occurring, and it felt good.

SOMETIMES, TOM ASKED me to help with the laundry. I couldn't imagine doing it on my own—I couldn't understand how the buttons on the machines worked.

"Here, let me show you again," he said, walking me through the steps. Each time he did laundry after that, he showed me the process, and little by little, it became familiar.

One day, I picked up the basket of dirty clothes with purpose.

"I'll come help you," Tom said.

I shook my head. "No. I've got it."

In the laundry room, I dumped the clothes on the floor and stared at the intimidating pile. When I loaded the washer and pushed the buttons, I felt a thrill—I'd done it!

Then I sat down to watch TV ... and promptly forgot all about the laundry.

Later, Tom said, "Mary, the washer stopped. Time to move things to the dryer. Want help?"

"Nope," I said with confidence.

I opened the washer, pulled out the clothes—and froze. The white underwear had turned pink.

When I told Tom, he chuckled.

"The colors bleed," he said. "Just wash the whites again with bleach."

I stared at him. "What's bleach?"

Gradually, I was doing more of the things Tom said I used to do. I wanted to remember what I was doing and told myself that I could.

Thank you, Lord, for helping me get better.

DAYS LATER, I tackled the laundry again.

Everything went smoothly until I removed a yellow blouse from the dryer and looked for a yellow hanger. There weren't any, so I went to our closet. I spotted one with a blue shirt hanging on it.

I snatched the hanger with the shirt on it and marched into the living room where Tom sat watching TV.

"Why is there a blue shirt on a yellow hanger?" I demanded, waving it around in a frenzy.

He looked at me like I was from another planet. "Mary, it doesn't make any difference what color the hanger is."

I stared at him, astonished. "Of course it does!"

"No, honey, it doesn't. We've been through this before. Matching hangers to the clothes doesn't matter."

"It matters to me. You know I need them to match."

"You didn't do that before you hit your head, and you don't need to do it now."

I felt my breath catch. "This is important to me!"

He sat up straighter. "Yes, I know, but it's unnecessary. And it wastes time. Can't you see that?"

"NO, I can't!" I stomped my foot. "Why can't you see I need the hangers and clothes to match?"

Why is he being so stubborn?

"But darling, it's not necessary—"

"If you don't agree, that's too bad! You need to do this."

"Mary, I'm not going to do that." He shook his head. "We can put the clothes on any color hanger."

I shook the yellow hanger and blue shirt at him. "No, Tom," I yelled, "I can't!"

My chest tightened as I stripped the blue shirt from the hanger, threw it on the couch, and slid the yellow one on the hanger. I held it up like proof, letting it speak for itself.

"See? This is the way it has to be. I'm not going to change."

"You never did this before your TBI. Why are you doing it now?"

"I don't know. I can't help it. It's just the way I am."

He threw his hands in the air. "Well, I can't keep up with all your ridiculous changes!"

He strode out of the room, and I dropped onto the couch. Fuming. Still gripping the yellow shirt on the yellow hanger. When the bedroom door slammed, I jumped.

I didn't know why he couldn't understand that I was trying to make sense of the world around me, and put things in order.

Twenty minutes later, he returned to the living room with a sheepish expression on his face. He apologized for getting so frustrated and sat down beside me. Putting his arms around me, he pulled me close.

I'd had time to think while he was in the other room, and had realized my new black-and-white way of seeing things could be hard for him. But that didn't change the fact I needed the clothes to match the hangers.

"I'm sorry too," I said.

"Let's go to Target and buy more hangers," he said.

I perked up, not believing my ears. I beamed at him, practically bouncing on the sofa. "Oh, thank you!"

At the store, I placed two bundles of multicolored hangers into our basket. Tom promptly removed them and put in two bundles of white ones.

"These are the only ones we need," he said.

I stared at him in surprise. "But, Tom—"

"We need to use only white hangers for all the clothes from now on," he said.

No, that's not what I want.

"Tom, I don't know if I can do that. I thought—"

"You can. This'll make everything easier, Mary. It's the best answer."

I sighed dramatically, resisting the urge to argue again. I didn't reply out loud, but in my head, I was already matching all the clothes to the hangers.

I'm going to hang clothes on any hanger I want.

Tom smiled like he'd won. "Great," he said. "Now that that's settled, there's another little habit you need to change that also started after your TBI."

I raised an eyebrow. "Oh really?"

"You don't have to group all the clothes together by color when you hang them in the closet."

I blinked. "I can't stop doing that."

I felt like stomping my foot again, but instead, I folded my arms across my chest and glared at him.

He must've realized my determination because, after a moment, he surrendered. "Okay. It was just an idea."

"Yeah," I said sweetly, "a bad one." I would hang the clothes anywhere I wanted to.

Back home, I continued doing the laundry, on my terms. It gave me a sense of accomplishment.

Tom started calling the laundry room my "office," and it was funny. When mysterious white spots appeared on our clothes, he joked there was a spot monster living in my office, and I banned myself from using bleach.

AS MARY'S NEW way of thinking continued to unfold, I accepted that life with her could take surprising turns. Nothing was routine anymore—every day held the potential for both wonder and discovery.

I began guiding her into new situations, offering her fresh opportunities to explore, process information, and make choices. And the more she did, the stronger and faster her thinking became, and her confidence bloomed.

One day, I took her on a date to an amusement park. This was a new experience in her mind—she didn't remember the times we'd been to one before. The park buzzed with life, busy with children, adults, clowns, rides, music, and entertainment. Mary slipped her hand into mine as we wandered around, wide-eyed and laughing, enjoying the magic of the park.

We snacked on cotton candy as we mingled with the crowd, and then, after playing some arcade games, Mary saw the roller coaster. She got so excited by the idea of riding it, I let her convince me to ride it with her. She couldn't remember I didn't like roller coasters, and I didn't tell her. Despite my unease with riding it, her excitement made it fun. As she rode, she screamed with the abandon of someone relearning how to feel alive.

The sun dipped low, and we ended our date by riding on the Ferris wheel. We held hands as we rose above the world. She beamed at me, eyes sparkling with joy, and I promised to bring her back on another day. Another date. Another chance for her to build a memory.

BY THIS POINT after my accident, I could sometimes remember big blocks of memory better. I remembered driving Tom to the medical clinic after a dinner out made him sick, and I remembered learning how to drive when I was fifteen. I had gotten my learner's permit, but Dad's truck had a clutch, and Mom didn't want me to drive her car. So when Joe came by our parents' house one day to see Dad, and Mom and Dad weren't home, I asked him to teach me how to drive.

"Mary," he asked, "have you ever driven?"

"No, but I have to start sometime, and I could drive your car if you'll teach me." He owned a green Malibu that was two years old.

"Okay," he said, "but don't tell anyone."

I drove us to Sonic Drive-In. We ordered a meal, and then I drove us back. That day motivated me to get a job so I could buy my own car when I turned sixteen.

Two weeks later, I started working as a waitress. I took every shift I could get, and by sixteen, I had the down payment for a new car I had picked out. It was a plum-purple Plymouth Barracuda with a white leather interior and white vinyl top. I loved that car. My friends at school loved it too—so much that they often rented it from me during lunch hour so they could drive it around. That Barracuda made me very popular.

I GRABBED MY morning coffee and stepped onto the back porch. Tom was already there with his coffee mug, soaking in the sunshine. I claimed my seat in the chair beside him and took a long breath.

"I want to start driving again," I said.

His head turned sharply. "Mary, you don't need to." His voice held a note of concern I knew well. "I'll take you anywhere you want to go."

"I know," I said gently. "But I want to drive."

He shook his head. "That's not a good idea."

"I think I'm ready."

"Are you sure?" he asked. "Maybe you need to give yourself more time."

I stared intently at him. He didn't speak for a minute, but I could tell his mind was turning over the idea. Finally, he nodded.

"Okay," he said. "But only if you go to a driving school that's supervised by a doctor. If they say it's safe for you to drive, fine. But if not, then you can't do it."

"Ok. I'll do it," I said.

Tom found a school, and I went. I attended for two full days and passed. I walked outside, waving my certificate like a flag of freedom.

"I'll drive us home," I said.

"No," Tom said.

"What? Why not?"

"Because it's not safe."

I stared at him. "But I passed the class!"

As he drove us home, I sat in the passenger seat trying not to let frustration take over my emotions.

"Tom, the accident already took enough from me. Don't you see? I only have right now, each day. Yes, it's scary for me to drive, but I want to. And I want you to help me."

He glanced at me, clearly torn. "Then we need to try another class."

I groaned. "Another one?"

"Yes. You have a TBI, and I need to be sure you know the rules of the road, and how to navigate traffic. Driving is dangerous. I need to know you're safe."

So I went. And again, I passed.

When I came out smiling and handed him the certificate, he didn't look at it. I asked him to move to the passenger seat so I could drive us home. He didn't budge.

"I'm proud of you, Mary, but I'm still too afraid for you to drive."

I rolled my eyes. "What do I need to do to convince you?"

"If you really want to do this, let me find one more class."

"Seriously?"

"I promise if you pass it, I won't ask you to go to another one, and I'll support your driving."

I attended another class and passed again.

And finally, Tom agreed to let me drive.

As I sat in the driver's seat, he ran through the steps to make sure I knew what to do. He hated that I was driving, but I loved it.

"Watch out!" he shouted as I wove between the curb and the yellow line. His hand slapped the dashboard like it could halt the car.

Despite his worry, I was excited. I was behind the wheel again. If my accident had taught me anything, it was how temporary life is. It's only a wisp, here today and gone before you know it. I wanted to really live, and with each new skill I acquired, I felt more alive.

For weeks, I only drove with Tom in the car. Our trips were short.

Once I'd gotten over my initial fear, driving had become lots of fun for me, but Tom was still beside himself with worry, afraid that I would get hurt again.

Eventually, I knew it was time for the next step—to venture out on my own.

"Tom, I want to go to the mall," I told him one morning.

"Sure," he said casually. "When?"

"By myself."

He blinked rapidly. "What? Why don't you want me to go?"

I smiled. "I think it's time to drive on my own."

He sighed. "Mary, you don't have to do this—"

"But I want to. I need it."

He hesitated, then gave me that long, worried look—the one that said he wanted to keep me safe more than anything.

"Well, I don't like it, but I guess it has to happen sooner or later. Promise me, Mary, you will be very, very careful."

I grinned. "I will."

He looked at me like he'd never see me again, and gave me a tender kiss on the cheek, followed by a tight hug.

"You can let me go now, Tom." I laughed.

"Right." He let go and laughed nervously. "Drive careful."

I smiled, said I would, and headed out the door. The mall was five miles away. I made it without incident and called Tom the moment I parked, as promised, to let him know I'd arrived safely. After some window shopping and a snack, I called again to say I was heading home.

When I pulled up to the house, Tom was outside, waiting.

As I got out of the car, he opened his arms, and I grinned and stepped right into them. He didn't say anything—but he didn't have to. I knew it had been hard for him to let me go, even for just a few hours. But he did it. He loved me enough to hold on tight ... and enough to let me go.

43

Cooking Again

While Tom prepared dinner, I sat in the living room flipping through one of the new magazines he'd bought me.

Reading was beyond me, but I enjoyed the pictures. Page after page, women smiled from the kitchens, stirring pots, holding out food. I set the magazine down and walked into the kitchen.

"Tom," I asked softly, "am I supposed to be cooking?"

He looked up from the stove, a spoon in hand. "Why do you ask?"

"In those magazines ... a lot of women are cooking."

He smiled. "You used to do most of the cooking. Before the accident."

"Was I good at it?"

"Oh yes. You loved it. And we loved cooking together."

"Then I want to do it again."

He hesitated. "Mary, that's not necessary."

"But I want to."

He set the spoon down and turned to face me fully.

"Darling, I like cooking for you. You should let me keep doing it."

I met his eyes. "But you've been telling me to try things I used to do. Why not this?"

He looked around slowly, then nodded. "All right. You want to start now?"

I smiled. "Yes."

He handed me a box from the counter. "Here's the stuffing. You can help me make it."

"How?"

He resumed stirring. "You need to get a cup of water."

I reached for a coffee mug.

With a chuckle, he said "No," and handed me a glass container with red writing printed on the side.

"This is a measuring cup." He pointed to the writing. "Fill the cup with water to that mark."

I did as he said. "Now what?"

He nudged a pan toward me. "Pour it in there."

One step at a time, he walked me through making the meal. It would've been easier for him to do it all himself, but he didn't. He stood beside me, patient, letting me find my way.

When we finished, the kitchen smelled like home.

And for the first time I could remember, I felt like I belonged in it.

I was gradually pulling my life back together, and with every victory, my confidence kept building.

A LOUD CRASH shattered the silence somewhere deep in the house.

My heart jolted.

Is Mary okay?

Steeling myself for whatever lay ahead, I rushed toward the sound. She stood motionless in the dining room, beside a glittering scatter of glass shards on the floor. At first glance, she seemed unhurt.

"Are you all right?"

Mary stared down at the glass fragments, then gave a small nod.

"I'm fine, but that bowl ..." Her voice wavered. "It's like my life—shattered into pieces, with no way to put it back together."

She looked up at me, tears in her eyes.

The victim was a beautiful crystal bowl. A wedding present.

"Don't worry about the bowl," I said, trying to soothe her. "It was an accident."

I grabbed a broom and dustpan from the closet and swept up the shards.

"I'm sorry, Tom."

"Sweetheart, nothing matters as much as you do." I set the broom and dustpan aside and pulled her gently into my arms. "You're not hurt, and that's what matters." I kissed the top of her head. "Your life isn't like that bowl. You're getting better, Mary. It's slow, but it's happening. And that bowl—" I shrugged. "It's just a bowl. You're what's important."

THE NEXT DAY, Mary showed me a handwritten recipe she'd found in a kitchen drawer. I hesitated for a moment, caught off guard.

Chicken Delight. The title was written in her delicate handwriting. I pointed to the title and chuckled. "That's my favorite meal. We call it Chicken Delight. It's a delicious casserole you created."

"I want to try making it with you," she said, her voice laced with hope.

The thought of her cooking made my chest tighten. It wasn't that I didn't want to help her, but—the idea of her in the kitchen again felt like too much, too soon. She'd helped with small things in the kitchen a few times recently, but this? Returning to cooking? I felt like she wasn't ready for it.

"Oh, darling, you're sweet, but I don't mind cooking for us."

She looked crestfallen. I knew it would be simpler for me to handle the cooking alone, but I also knew it was crucial to support and encourage her. And I couldn't stand to see her deflated. I loved her so much and wanted her to be happy. I took a deep breath.

"Okay," I said with a smile. "If you really want to try to learn to cook again, I'll help you. But we'll have to take it slow."

Her eyes lit up, that soft, hopeful gleam returning. She nodded enthusiastically, and I felt a warmth fill me that was both comforting and unsettling.

We sat down at the kitchen table, and I made the conversation light. I explained the process of making the casserole, keeping things simple, step by step. It felt almost playful. She agreed to let me do all the chopping and cutting.

"Are you ready?" I asked.

She paused, then smiled. "I think so."

As we mixed the ingredients, I couldn't help but feel the romance of working side by side in the kitchen again. There were some moments of frustration, but cooking together felt right, like the world was opening up just a bit more. When she got something wrong, I soothed her feelings and lovingly teased her.

"Darling, you're the greatest cook in the world." She lightly chuckled.

Finally, the meal was prepared.

"We did it!" Mary exclaimed, her voice filled with pride.

I smiled, taking a bite. "This is scrumptious, sweetheart. Just like you used to make it."

We stared at each other for a frozen moment, then burst into loud laughter. The idea that she could cook without help—lots of it—was hilarious. Laughing had never felt so good.

Her eyes sparkled with joy.

"I love the sound of your laughter, Mary," I said softly. "I've missed it."

I hadn't heard it nearly enough since the accident. But hearing it now, so happy, so full of life, reminded me of how our home used to feel—filled with joy, lightness, and love. And here we were, moving forward, taking back pieces of what we had lost.

With the satisfaction radiating from her, I knew cooking again could be an important step in her recovery. It was about pulling herself back together, and with each victory, she was doing it, step by step.

"TOM, WHAT DID I do in my spare time before the accident?"

He glanced up from his desk. "You were an avid reader."

I hadn't been able to read since the accident, but something inside me stirred at the thought. If reading had been part of who I was before, maybe I could do it again.

"Will you get me something to read that I'd like?"

He hesitated, his brow furrowing. "I've been getting you magazines from the grocery store, but you've only been looking at the pictures. You should try to read the articles."

He bought me several more magazines, including a copy of *Reader's Digest* with large print. I flipped through the pages, but only the pictures made sense.

In a quiet voice, I reminded Tom that I couldn't read.

"Let me help," he said. He started reading the articles to me, pointing to the words as he spoke them. His voice was steady, like a lifeline in the middle of a storm. I wanted to join in, but couldn't—all I saw on the pages were splotches of ink.

"Mary, you can do this," he encouraged.

"What kind of books did I like?"

"Fiction. Mystery and suspense bestsellers."

"Can you get me one?"

He bought me a book, and I sat down, opened it, and looked at the pages. Nothing made any sense. I looked again, hoping for some miracle to unlock the meaning, but I couldn't make heads or tails of what I was seeing.

"Tom, is this in English?"

He looked curiously at me. "Yes, why?"

"I can't read it."

He walked over, looked down at the book I held, and smiled. He took it from my hands, turned it over, and handed it back with a soft smile. "There you go," he said, and kissed my forehead. "That's how you read it."

I blinked. "I didn't even know it was upside down," I muttered.

"It's okay," he assured me, his hand gently brushing my hair. "You just need to be patient. Things will keep coming back to you."

I nodded, but doubt clouded my mind. I opened the book again. Everything looked like gibberish.

"I can't do this," I whispered, feeling defeated.

Tom had me set the book aside. "Try the *Reader's Digest* again."

I couldn't read it either, so he began reading it to me again. He read it to me over several days, and as he did, I interrupted him with lots of questions. We had lengthy conversations about reading, and he encouraged me to believe in the importance of learning do it again.

I tried again, but it was impossible. With every failed attempt, my frustration grew. I wondered if maybe I'd never remember how.

"In order to read," Tom said, "you must be calm. Try not to be frustrated, it interferes with reading. It's important that you learn to read again. You can do it. Keep trying."

I shook my head. "How can I be calm when—"

"Honey, you need to relax. Relax and concentrate. You can do this."

He seemed confident I could figure it out, and that inspired me to keep trying, but no matter how hard I tried, the words on the pages just didn't make sense.

Weeks passed. Tom kept reading to me, and telling me how helpful and fun reading was, but I still couldn't figure out written words. Then one day, I discovered there were a few words I recognized. I shared my discovery with Tom, and we discussed the importance of remembering all the words I could.

Tom kept encouraging me to believe I could read again, and that my memory would get better. He bought several books about how to improve memory and read them to me. We worked hard at doing the exercises, practicing every one of them in earnest.

A couple more weeks went by, and off and on, I continued trying to read. I'd gotten to where a few more words made sense, but I had begun to believe that I would never be able to read more than that.

AS WE WENT about our daily activities, Tom continued pushing my memory, attempting to make it stronger.

He tested me with questions and turned it into a game. He told me that I had to remember the things that happened around us each day, and later that day, he would ask me what those things were.

The game was a lot of fun, but often, remembering what he asked about was a giant task I couldn't complete.

"What coffee mug did you use for breakfast this morning?" he would ask, or "Who did we say hello to on our walk today?"

Then he began asking me about things that had happened the previous day. That was even more difficult to remember. Sometimes, we burst out laughing at my answers.

Occasionally, I passed his tests, but more often, I didn't. Once, he told me that I had failed a test, and that I would have to repeat it later. It was so hilarious—we couldn't stop laughing.

Slowly, the balance was shifting, and my wins were starting to outweigh the losses.

WE DISCUSSED READING often, and Tom answered all my questions. I kept trying to do it, but I became convinced it was just another mountain I couldn't climb. It felt futile, and I was too frustrated to keep trying.

I marched into Tom's office, threw back my shoulders, took a deep breath, and announced, "I can't do it."

"Can't do what?"

"Read. I'm never going to learn how. And I'm finished trying. Seeing the pictures is enough."

He smiled gently. "Darling, the more you practice, the easier it'll get."

I whirled around in a huff and stalked out. Later, I calmed down and found myself questioning what Tom had said. Did he really think I could learn to read again? I felt sure I couldn't. But deep down, I wanted to make him happy, so I pushed aside my frustration and tried again. I struggled hard to figure it out. Tom had faith in me. Maybe that was enough to keep me going.

One day, as I was struggling to figure out a jumble of words, I asked Tom again, "Why should I learn to read?"

"There's lots of reasons. You used to love reading. Stories take you to another place. It's fun, and you can learn things."

With my weak memory not retaining much, I didn't see the point of trying to read. I felt sure that even if I did learn how, I wouldn't be able to remember what I read.

I decided I really didn't care about reading and tried to convince Tom, but he kept urging me to try.

For him, I kept at it. He had faith in me, and I didn't want to let him down.

Then slowly, my efforts made progress. Words became a little more familiar. The satisfaction of figuring them out was small, but it felt good.

Gradually, I began understanding more how words worked with other words, and phrases started making a little sense. And my memory started to work a little better.

Tom never stopped encouraging me to read better, and eventually, I started trying to decode short sentences. The satisfaction of making sense of written words was thrilling, but when I tried to put one sentence together with another one, I still couldn't do it—by the time I got to the end of a sentence, I had already forgotten the beginning of it.

But I knew I was making progress. "I'm getting it," I told myself.

AS I SAT in my recliner trying to read my book, it suddenly hit me: I was starting to understand sentences better—*I'm doing it!* But reading and remembering more than a couple of sentences at once remained a huge obstacle. My mind could only take in a small amount of information at a time.

I told Tom about my progress, my voice tinged with excitement. He smiled, encouraging me.

"You've got this, Mary. Believe in yourself. Reading will open new doors in your life, which can lead to more good things."

He also said that I was a stubborn person and that I could stick with trying to read until I figured it out.

Am I stubborn enough to learn to read again?

The idea of reading had gotten under my skin, and I became determined to get good at it. I wasn't about to quit.

ONE AFTERNOON, TOM asked, "Mary, do you remember Dr. Strider?"

"Yes."

We had met with him several times after the accident, and he had written the evaluation report about my brain injury.

"Do you remember he suggested you write down your thoughts and feelings? Because it would help you?"

"No."

"He said writing about things would help you understand them."

Tom handed me a book. "I bought you this journal. If you want, I think you might like writing things down and keeping a record."

I turned the journal over in my hands. "That's an interesting idea."

Trying to read was still a huge challenge for me. I wasn't sure I could learn how to write again too.

It felt like yet another mountain to climb.

44

A New Crisis

Four Years After

One afternoon, as we sat in the living room watching TV, a sudden wave of nausea hit me. I threw up, then passed out. Moments later, I woke, confused, then it happened again.

I woke and cried out frantically, "Tom, what's happening?"

"I don't know—"

It struck again, and when I woke, I fought though the panic filling me and yelled, "TOM!"

Before he could answer, it happened again.

The next thing I knew, Tom was rushing me to the ER.

I was admitted and given IV fluids and medicine to stop the nausea. The doctors ran lots of tests, but couldn't diagnose the cause. They kept me overnight.

On the second day, a doctor said, "You're stable now, and I can't find anything wrong. I'm sending you home."

Tom objected fervently, informing the doctor about several episodes the medical staff hadn't seen.

"There's nothing else we can do," the doctor replied, shaking his head.

That night, back at home, it happened again.

On the third day, we returned to the ER, and once again, they admitted me, gave me IV fluids and medicine, and were unable to diagnose the problem.

On the fourth day, they sent me home again, and the episodes continued.

On the fifth day, when the problem persisted, Tom called Dr. Anderson in desperation. He told us to return to the ER, promising to call ahead and ensure they kept me until they diagnosed the problem.

The admission was quick. My hospital stay wasn't. The episodes continued as the doctors ran every conceivable test, but still no answers.

The days turned into weeks. My appetite had vanished, along with my hope. I was sick of being sick and stressed to my limit.

AFTER THREE LONG, hard weeks in the hospital, I was drained and worn out. I started feeling like I would never leave the hospital.

Tom's worry was unmistakable—his usual cheer replaced by deep concern.

He held my hand and prayed. "Lord, we're sorry we have so many problems. We can't do this without you. Please help us. Please heal my dear wife. She's so sick, it's too much. I give you all our problems. Please open the doors we need to go through and give Mary the help she needs. We pray for your will to be done and trust you with everything. Thank you. Amen."

IN THE FOURTH week of my hospital stay, a new doctor stepped into my room.

"I'm a cardiologist," he said, "and I've reviewed your chart, seen all the test results. I know what the problem is. You need a pacemaker. Your passing out is due to a heart conduction problem. I've scheduled surgery for tomorrow morning."

I was stunned.

Tom peppered him with questions, but I couldn't keep up with the conversation. The doctor's answers sounded detailed, but he seemed rushed, as if he was already moving on to the next patient.

As the doctor turned to leave, like everything was already decided, Tom said, "Wait. I need more information."

The doctor spun around, but instead of answering Tom's questions, he pushed him to agree to surgery. Tom persisted.

After answering several more questions, the doctor asked Tom, "So, shall we proceed with the surgery?"

Tom shook his head. "No. I don't agree to it yet."

The doctor stared at him. "Why not?"

"Because I need to research further."

The air prickled with tension. "And why do you think you can make this decision for her?"

"Because I'm her husband."

The doctor's eyes narrowed. "How do you know she wants what you're saying?"

"Because I know her. And I'll let you know tomorrow what we've decided."

Tom held the doctor's gaze. The doctor pushed a few more times, but Tom was adamant.

Finally, the doctor shook his head and walked out.

"What do you think?" I asked Tom, my voice weak.

"I'll go home tonight and do more research on the internet."

He smiled as he straightened my covers.

I managed a faint smile in return.

BACK AT HOME that evening, worrying about Mary, I scoured the internet for hours. I researched everything she was experiencing, and what the cardiologist had said about her heart.

Between searches, I begged God for help.

Lord, please give me insight and wisdom to help Mary. Please tell me what the problem is. Please heal her mind and body. Help her get her health back. Please help me be strong for her and take good care of her. I give you all these problems and pray for your will. Thank you for helping us.

EARLY THE NEXT morning, Tom walked into my room wearing an expression of hope.

"Darling, last night I searched the internet and prayed hard for the answer to the problem, and I have an idea of what it might be."

"Oh?" I whispered, unable to speak louder.

He reminded me that a week before the episodes started, one of my doctors had prescribed a new medication, for pain.

"During my research and praying last night, it occurred to me that that might be what's making you sick. So, when the nurse brings all your pills today, I don't want you to take that one."

I stared blankly. "What?"

"Mary, don't take that pill."

"But Tom, I have to. The doctor prescribed it."

"No, you don't have to. They can't make you. And if that's why you're throwing up, then you shouldn't. So don't."

"But how?"

"When the nurse brings all your pills, tell them you don't want to take that one."

"I can't do that." I wanted to please him, but I couldn't imagine how I could do what he was saying.

"Okay," he said gently. "Then take all the other pills, but don't swallow that one. Put it in your mouth last, and only pretend to swallow it. After the nurse leaves, take it out and give it to me."

I trusted Tom, and desperate to get better, I did what he wanted.

The entire day, I wasn't nauseated, didn't throw up, and didn't pass out. It was a relief. The doctors and nurses had no idea what we'd done.

THE NEXT MORNING, Tom sat on the edge of my bed, his expression solemn.

"Darling, I hate to tell you this," he began quietly, "but when the nurse brings all your pills today, you need to take that pill again."

Alarm shot through me. "Why?"

"Because if you take it and get sick again, we'll know for sure that's the problem."

I hated the idea. If he was right, I'd be throwing up and passing out again.

I took the pill that morning, and all day long, the episodes happened. Misery returned full force. The medical staff was at a loss.

The next day, Tom stopped me from taking the pill again, and once more, I didn't get sick all day.

When the cardiologist came in to see me the next day, Tom told him, "I've figured out what was making her sick."

"Oh really. What?" The doctor sounded skeptical.

Tom explained what we had done.

"It can't be that pill," the doctor said flatly.

"Why not?" Tom asked.

"Because that's not one of the known side effects."

"It may not be a side effect for anyone else, but it is for her," Tom said, pointing at me.

Without saying anything, the doctor turned and left.

"He's not convinced," I murmured.

"That's okay," Tom replied calmly. "You're not taking that medicine anymore, so you won't be getting sick again. That's what matters. And you're coming home."

THE NEXT DAY, Tom got me released from the hospital and took me home.

I stepped on the scale and found I'd lost thirty-eight pounds during the five weeks I took that pill.

When I told Tom, he said with a wry smile, "That was a terrible diet plan."

Reflecting on the pain pill experience, I was glad to be past it and glad to be alive. During those dark days, Tom had been my strength, representing my best interest—even when I didn't know what that was, and I realized how important it is to have a supportive advocate who is both compassionate and logical when things are difficult.

I couldn't understand why the doctors hadn't solved the problem, but I was thankful Tom did. If not for him, I would've ended up with a pacemaker I didn't need—and would've continued throwing up, getting weaker, and heading down a much worse path.

Lord, thank you for my husband. Thank you that he takes good care of me. I know you're always with us, thank you. Please help me get healthier and help me be the best person I can be.

45

Spaghetti Noodles

"I've hired a house cleaner to come to our home," I told Mary one morning. "When she arrives, you need to tell her what you want done."

I saw uncertainty in her eyes as she glanced around the living room.

"How do I do that?" she asked.

I gave a small shrug. "Just tell her what you want cleaned and how you like it done."

"What if she doesn't understand me?" she murmured.

"She will. And I'll be here to help if you need me. But you can do this." I smiled. I wanted her to believe in herself. We talked about it more, and I gently emphasized she should try to manage this all on her own. I knew this could be a small step toward something bigger for her.

When the woman arrived, Mary stood up straight and, with a deep breath, took her from room to room, explaining what she wanted done. I trailed behind, just in case—ready to step in if things went sideways. But it wasn't necessary, Mary handled things like a champ, her words flowing easily. It was like watching her return to herself, and it warmed my heart.

After the woman finished cleaning, we walked from room to room, to make sure everything was how Mary liked it. She lingered in the rooms, her gaze moving around, as if taking in the difference.

"It's so clean," she said, a smile tugging at her lips.

But it wasn't just the gleaming floors or the dust-free shelves that made her smile. The house was clean—but more than that, Mary had taken control and reclaimed a piece of herself. And in that moment, a bold new confidence sparked in her eyes.

"She did exactly what you asked, and she'll be back next week to do it again. I'm so proud of you, darling," I said, my voice filled with admiration.

She beamed and threw her arms around me. "I love you!"

I held her close, deep satisfaction flooding me. It wasn't about the clean house, it was about Mary's progress, the connection between us, the trust, the quiet triumph we had shared.

MY MEMORY WAS still an immense roadblock, but I could tell it was growing. It wasn't happening quick, but the small wins were accumulating.

One afternoon, I asked Tom to help clarify my thoughts about an issue. I needed to find a way to connect the dots about something.

"Thoughts can be like spaghetti," he said, smiling, his voice warm with humor.

"What?"

"Trains of thought are like spaghetti noodles," he said, as if it made perfect sense.

I couldn't help but laugh.

"For someone without a TBI, the noodles are lined up straight and neat, like spaghetti in a box. But for someone with a TBI, the noodles are like cooked spaghetti—tangled and twisted. Your noodles just need some straightening."

He smiled, as if he had just solved a riddle for me.

I laughed again, appreciating his lighthearted analogy. It was a funny way to think about thoughts, and it made sense, but deep down, I wanted more than just untangled thoughts. I wanted to think faster, to understand more, and to remember better.

As I pressed him for more, he simply encouraged me to keep figuring things out. It wasn't the answer I'd sought, but the way he smiled and looked at me made me feel more confident I could find it on my own.

I KEPT TRYING to read, hoping I'd get better at it. Every sentence was a puzzle, and I was forced to reread over and over to make any sense of it. Since I still saw four of everything, I focused on the image at the far-right, the one I knew was real.

I pushed myself to read beyond what I felt my memory could hold. I worked hard to retain everything, trying to stretch my memory like it was a muscle in a tight knot.

My slow progress aggravated me, but I refused to give up, and bit by bit, the amount I could read and remember slowly grew. As I began to understand how sentences worked, my ability to comprehend them improved, and I started to grasp paragraphs a little, but still, I had to keep rereading to make anything stick in my memory.

I RECEIVED A call from my sister Kate, who lived in Oklahoma. I couldn't recall the last time we'd spoken, but hearing her voice brought a smile to my lips. She was one year older, and we had always been close growing up.

"Mary," she began, "I care about you, and I have some questions I want to ask if that's okay."

"Sure," I said, settling into my recliner.

As she talked, I realized that someone had given her incorrect information about a conversation in the past—one I clearly remembered. I shared the facts with Kate, but she still didn't understand.

I tried again. "Kate, you've been given some wrong information. I've forgotten a lot of things, but I remember this. There was a conversation where I was spoken to hatefully, about the brain injury."

Kate sighed on the other end of the line. "I was also told you're living in an alternate reality."

"I'm sorry you were told that, and I'm glad you called so I can tell you the truth. And Kate, it's never right to be hateful, to anyone."

"Why would they do that?" she asked, sounding confused.

"I don't know. Maybe they want attention. Some people will say anything. But now you know the truth. That's what matters."

"Then tell me, Mary, how are you doing?"

I smiled, considering the question. "Well, having a brain injury changes things."

"How so?"

"I look at everything in a different way."

We talked a little longer and agreed to stay in touch more.

After we hung up, I replayed the conversation in my mind, grateful I could remember and answer Kate's questions, grateful for those who cared about the truth. They were a blessing in my life.

Lord, thank you for being my Lord. I don't know how people who don't have a relationship with you can get by. I pray for all my family members. I pray for those who are hurting and hope they find peace and life through you. I know anything is possible with you and praise you for all your goodness. Thank you, Lord.

46

Endless Doors

Five Years After

Ever since the accident, I'd searched for the person I used to be, wanting to become her again. But gradually, I realized she was gone, and I had to figure out who I was now.

I kept asking Tom questions, anything that occurred to me, and he kept telling me everything he could. Yet, trying to understand the woman I had become was a big challenge, and I prayed for God's help.

Tom continued taking me on dates, and swept up in his affection and the excitement of our relationship, I found myself falling deeply in love. It felt both familiar and new at the same time. Whether we went out to eat, took a walk, or anything else, each date was special and brought us closer. Wanting our relationship to be based on who I was now, not on whoever I'd been before, I kept learning more about myself and about Tom.

One day, I realized my life was like a hallway lined with unopened doors—each one representing new choices, new possibilities. It was up to me to decide which ones to open.

I asked God to guide me to the right doors, and when I made a bad choice, to help me start over. Prayer gave me hope and confidence, but making decisions remained a big struggle.

I wanted to make only good decisions—choices that would help my life get better. I didn't know how much of my old abilities would return, but that didn't discourage me as much as it had before, and I kept trying to open the right doors—to figure out what puzzled me, and to make good choices.

Fear and uncertainty sometimes crept in, making it harder to be hopeful, but my strong will was an asset. I kept trying to mimic Tom's positive attitude, though I couldn't always do it. At times, failure frustrated me, but other times, it pushed me to try harder.

The roller coaster ride of my life continued, but the steep climbs and hard falls had become less frequent.

I shared my thoughts and feelings with Tom, wondering if they were unique to my brain's new way of thinking. He assured me that they were normal for everyone, not just brain injury survivors.

"Everyone makes choices and goes through ups and downs," he said. "We're all in control of what we think, and say, and do. That includes what we don't think, say, or do. It just looks a little different for you. And a person's responsibility exists whether they like it or not, and whether they know it or not."

"I don't understand. What responsibility?"

"We're all responsible for our own decisions. You, me, the children, and everyone else. You make your decisions, and they have consequences. And you're responsible for those consequences, and for how you choose to deal with them. You create your life through your choices, so you need to be careful and make the best ones you can."

At first, I didn't comprehend what he said, so we talked it through again. He encouraged me to keep facing my choices and trying to make the best ones possible.

I thought about Dylan and Cody. Having a head injury hadn't been my choice, but accepting it was. It had been hard for me to accept, which made me more understanding toward the two boys, but if they wanted to see me, they had to accept it too. Until then, I'd miss being part of their lives, and they'd miss being part of mine. I knew they were no longer little children and made their own decisions, but it was uncomfortable to think they didn't want to be part of my life. The empty spot in my heart remained, but my faith in God gave me peace.

Tom read another scripture to me: "If God is for us, who can be against us?"[8]

"MARY," TOM SAID, "I think it's time we return to church for a Sunday morning service."

I paused. The thought of that made me anxious. "I'm not sure I can," I said.

---

[8] Romans 8:31

He smiled gently. "I know you can. You've made so much progress since the last time we tried, you can do it. I think it would be good for us, and I'd like us to go next Sunday. Will you do that?"

"Where would we go?"

"To the little Baptist church that's three miles away. You know the one. We've driven past it many times."

"I don't know."

"Okay, how about this. Let's go there sometime this week and just meet with the pastor. We can walk through the church and see what it looks like."

That sounded all right, and a few days later we drove to the church. I was quiet on the way there, unsure what to expect. As we walked inside, Tom took my hand, and it felt a little like we were on a date. His quiet confidence dissolved my uncertainty.

We didn't have an appointment, but the pastor, a middle-aged man who was kind and reassuring, welcomed us with a friendly smile. As we walked through the building with him, chatting, I felt myself lighten up and we even laughed with him a little.

I couldn't remember the last time I'd attended a church service, but I was starting to think I might like it.

DAYS LATER, I found myself thinking about some things that I'd learned since the accident, including how fragile and fleeting life is. We're all only a heartbeat, a single breath, away from death, and it could happen any moment. That was abundantly clear to me, and I wanted to use whatever time I had left carefully.

Instead of allowing my thoughts to be filled with fear and anxiety, I wanted to fill my thoughts with faith, hope, and love. Negative thinking had caused insecurity, and now, I wanted to fill my mind with thoughts of God and the principles in the Bible. I remembered it was the path I had been on before the accident, and I knew I was becoming who I wanted to be. That knowledge gave me comfort, and I trusted God to keep helping me.

As I sat thinking, the accident suddenly returned in a flash—

BANG! The car spinning ... crashing ... a slow-motion sensation ... walking down a hallway ... a bright light, warm and inviting ... love filling me ... I saw my dad and Jesus ...

"I want to be in heaven," I told Jesus.

Jesus spoke to me.

"I don't understand," I replied.

"You will," he said.

And then, just like that, the memory stopped.

What did Jesus tell me? Come on, Mary, think! Think!

But no matter how hard I tried, that piece of memory eluded me.

I found Tom and told him what I'd remembered. As I filled him in, the words flowed from me. He listened intently.

"That's great, Mary, but what did Jesus say?"

"I'm trying to remember. It was something important."

"Well, give yourself more time."

TOM CONTINUED URGING me to try reading. I kept at it, slowly at first, but gradually I got better—and more of what I read began to stick. One paragraph. Then another. As paragraphs grew easier, my new goal became reading and remembering an entire page. Still, I kept flipping pages back and forth, rereading over and over.

Tom teased me good-naturedly: "It's funny to watch you flipping through the pages."

His comment made me want to try even harder. I pushed myself to solve the puzzle of reading and remembering. My memory was inconsistent, but reading helped it improve. And as it did, the messages in the words started making more sense.

Reading and remembering became a mystery I was compelled to solve. Eventually, I could sometimes read an entire page without needing to reread it. What had once felt impossible now seemed possible.

My memory still didn't retain information for very long, but as I practiced reading, I could tell it was improving.

Reading one page turned into several. Several turned into chapters. And as I rediscovered the joy of reading, I pushed further and finished the entire book.

The feeling was wonderful. I still didn't read or remember as well as I wanted, but knowing I could read again was exhilarating.

Since I can do this, what else can I do?

47

Returning to Church

Most days, I lived in the blur between what I remembered and what I didn't. This morning was no different. I spotted my mug in the microwave, cold coffee inside, and couldn't remember if it was supposed to be my first cup or my second.

On the counter beside it lay a note in my handwriting. I didn't remember writing it. Tom had told me to try to write things down, to help me remember and think through my thoughts, but the words scribbled across the paper made no sense. I stared at them, hoping for something to click. It didn't.

What if this is as good as my memory ever gets?

I kept struggling to remember—old memories, new ones, everything. My memory was tricky. It was like a piece of Swiss cheese, full of holes. My forgetfulness was so bad that sometimes I forgot whether I was trying to recall an old memory or save a new one. Other times, I'd start to save something in my memory, only to forget what I wanted to remember. But I could tell my memory was getting a little better.

I accepted that I wouldn't remember everything, and told myself that not all things were worth holding onto. But the important things, those were what I needed most. Knowing the difference, though, wasn't easy.

ONE MORNING, TOM read this verse to me: "Whatever is true, whatever is noble, whatever is right, whatever is pure, whatever is lovely, whatever is admirable—if anything is excellent or praiseworthy—think about such things."[9]

I paused for a moment, letting the words seep into my mind. Scriptures were a great help. I rested in the comfort of what they said.

Lord, thank you for your love. Thank you for helping me heal.

Memories kept sliding in and out of my mind—there one day, gone the next, and then back again as if they'd never left.

Trying to use my memory was like trying to piece together a jigsaw puzzle with missing pieces, and not knowing which pieces were missing. And from day to day, the pieces that were missing kept changing. But some days, it almost felt like the picture made sense.

When the difficulties became too much, I did what strengthened me most: I placed everything in God's hands. I trusted him to make my life be what he wanted it to be.

---

[9] Philippians 4:8

IT HAD BEEN a month since our tour of the Baptist church, and I finally felt ready to return.

"Tom, I want to go to church again. The one we toured," I said.

He spun to face me and grinned. "That's great! Next Sunday?"

"Yes, but I'll need extra coffee before going," I smiled.

"We'll go out to breakfast first, to help you wake up," he said, pulling me into a hug.

When Sunday came, my nerves were humming. An older man with a kind smile greeted us at the door and handed us a bulletin. Inside, there were two tables on the left, and a man and woman stood behind them handing out cookies and cups of coffee. People were milling around, smiling and talking. The sanctuary felt welcoming and peaceful. Sunlight filtered through tall stained-glass windows on the sides. A larger window behind the stage showed Jesus, his arms open. The high cathedral ceiling gave the room an airy openness, while the light cream walls adorned with colorful scripture banners made the room feel warm and comfortable. Curved, padded rows of seating sloped gently toward the stage.

About three hundred people filled the sanctuary—some standing, others seated or moving around, their voices blending in hushed conversations. Families sat together, children fidgeting beside their parents, elderly couples holding hands. A few people glanced our way, offering warm smiles and nods of welcome. I was glad I'd chosen to wear my cheerful blue dress, the white polka dots making it feel lively.

How nice everyone looks.

As the lights dimmed, we found seats near the back. Tom unfolded the bulletin we'd been handed upon arriving and began to read. I was more interested in watching the people around us. Some still stood, chatting with those already seated, while others looked about, finding their seats. Soft piano music floated through the air, creating a comforting atmosphere, and I felt myself relaxing.

The pastor, who Tom reminded me had given us the church tour the month before, walked to the podium, and the room quickly fell silent. His deep voice resonated with warmth and conviction.

"Good morning, everyone. It's good to be in the house of the Lord. Please stand in his honor and pray with me."

Soon, the choir, dressed in golden robes, rose as one and began the familiar hymn "How Great Thou Art." The harmonies swelled, filling the sanctuary, and a lump formed in my throat. Memories of other Sundays in church surfaced— how much I'd loved attending, the comfort of the music, the quiet sense of belonging.

Tom reached for my hand, his grip steady and reassuring. I squeezed back, letting the warmth anchor me amid the swirl of memories and nerves.

The choir sang more songs. Listening to them, and the congregation singing along, brushed the edge of memories buried deep in my mind, and haltingly, I began to sing too.

The pastor spoke about faith and trusting God—his words simple, yet deeply moving. As I focused on the sermon, a steady calm settled over me.

"There are times when we hesitate, uncertain of the path before us," he said. "But God walks with us, even when we don't realize it."

I'd been unsure about coming here, about opening my heart to the church again. But sitting in the warm, welcoming space, listening to the uplifting sermon—it felt right, as if I'd found another piece of myself that had been lost.

I glanced at Tom. He gave a quiet, knowing smile, one that seemed to understand everything I was feeling.

When the service ended, we slipped out before the crowd. Stepping into the morning sunshine, I reached for Tom's hand, my heart light and grateful. I had made it through an entire Sunday service—a hurdle that had once felt impossible. It felt like a new beginning.

"How do you feel?" Tom asked.

I drew in a deep, steadying breath, letting the peace of the moment settle through me.

"Good," I said. "Really good."

He grinned. "Then let's come back again."

I nodded, certain in my heart we would.

48

Increasing Confidence

Six Years After

My memory was finally working much better. Sitting in the living room one day, I let my mind wander through the labyrinth of memories I'd recovered despite my head injury, and recalled my life as a child.

My dad had been 6'2", broad-shouldered and strong, and a loving father. Throughout my childhood, he held a family Bible study every evening during the week for about thirty minutes. He would read a passage of scripture, then everyone would share their thoughts. Dad was a mechanic who could repair anything. He spent the first half of his working life fixing large machinery: eighteen-wheelers, dump trucks, and Caterpillar tractors. Then he became a demolitions expert, toppling tall buildings with carefully placed explosives.

My mom, on the other hand, was only 5' tall, tiny standing beside Dad. She was a Christian woman, but also superstitious, with some really wild ideas. When I was about eight years old, she taught me that two people couldn't work on making up the same bed at the same time, or someone would get sick in it. I was just a little kid, and I believed everything she said. When I was thirteen, she warned me that walking on a gravesite would cause the person buried there to haunt my dreams while I slept. That time, I was certain Mom had lost her marbles.

Besides me, there were eight other siblings in our house, and it was a busy place. Mom believed in the Christian principle of turning the other cheek when someone did you wrong—but when it came to her children, she believed in "spare the rod and spoil the child." When we did something really bad, Mom would head into the backyard to a big willow tree and cut off a switch. She liked the ones about five feet long. She didn't use a willow switch often, but by the time I was seven, I'd learned to avoid the switch by doing whatever Mom said.

Dad taught us the importance of living a godly life; Mom taught us the importance of staying out of trouble. I always wanted to make them happy, and they shaped me into someone who always tried to be good.

As I reflected on my life, I was grateful for parents who had done their best to raise me. Now, with the knowledge of how fleeting life could be, I understood the importance of having the right priorities and my relationship with Christ was at the very top. When life became difficult, his strength comforted me.

Lord, thank you for your presence in my life. Thank you for people who love me. Please help me live the way you want me to. I trust and depend on you in everything. Amen.

I STILL MISSED talking with Mary the way I could before the accident, but she would always be my sweetheart. I cherished the new connection between us that enduring the injury together had brought about, and I loved the new person she'd become.

We kept returning to the little Baptist church. Mary couldn't manage regular attendance, so we usually went only once or twice a month. Still, attending lifted our spirits, and we genuinely enjoyed it.

After church one day, Dylan showed up at our home.

We hadn't seen him for a year, and for a moment, I wondered if he'd had a change of heart—if our relationship might improve. But he was only there to pick up some item he wanted from the garage.

He spent a few minutes talking with Mary in the living room before heading out to find the item.

After he found it, I asked, "Don't you think you might like to come visit Mom sometime?"

He looked down. "I don't know."

"Why not, Dylan?"

He hesitated. "It's hard to see her with the brain injury."

"Well, she misses you."

"Maybe I'll call her later," he said.

I watched him get into his car and drive away. Mary and I missed him, and Cody too. Mary was a smart, loving woman, and a mother to be proud of, but the relationship with the two boys was no longer the same.

THAT EVENING, I told Tom that I was going to call Dylan.

"Hi, it was good to see you today. I'm sorry you couldn't stay longer."

"Hey, Mom."

I invited him to come over for lunch sometime. He said he would try to.

Before I could think of how to respond, he said, "I have to go."

I heard the click as the call disconnected.

The boys' absence left a hollow ache in my chest. I went to Tom and said, "I don't understand why Dylan and Cody don't come see me more."

"They're uncomfortable with how the injury changed you."

I mulled that over for a moment. I knew some people were uncomfortable being around someone with an illness or injury—but for Dylan and Cody, I wasn't just anyone. I was their mother. I didn't understand why the head injury had affected our relationship.

"I love the boys and really miss them," I said, and I hoped that someday, they'd come back to me.

49

My New Normal

Seven Years After

Working with thinking challenges was my new normal. I turned to Tom with a question I couldn't shake.

He replied with a question of his own. "Do you know the story of the oyster and the pearl?"

"No."

"When an oyster lives in the ocean, sometimes a grain of sand gets inside its shell. The sand is rough and irritating to the oyster's thin, delicate skin. And since the oyster has no way to remove the sand, it reacts by secreting a fluid that coats it.

"And as the oyster keeps coating the sand with fluid, the sand gradually changes from rough to smooth. The oyster secretes layer after layer of fluid around it until eventually, the sand changes into a smooth, little ball that doesn't hurt the oyster anymore. That little ball is the pearl. The oyster continues to secrete fluid around it, and the ball keeps growing. And sooner or later, a person comes along and opens the oyster shell and finds the pearl inside. And that's where pearls come from."

"Really?"

"Yes. The oyster's shell and your skull are both hard, protective surfaces that guard what's inside, the oyster and your brain. Your brain injury is like a grain of sand that gets inside the oyster's shell.

"The grain of sand irritates the oyster just like the TBI irritates you. And just as the oyster coats the sand to make it more comfortable, you need to coat the TBI with your own kind of fluid to make the injury more comfortable for you."

"How do I do that?"

"You coat the injury with your thoughts, by the thinking you choose. Every thought you have creates your life. The more you think the right thoughts, the more comfortable the injury becomes. Just like the oyster turns the irritating sand into the pearl, you can think good thoughts that shape your life into something better. Do you understand?"

"I think so."

Tom leaned over and gently touched the side of my head. "We can't remove the injury from your head, just like the oyster can't remove the sand from its shell. So you need to work with the problem like the oyster does—by choosing the thoughts you need. It's important to choose the right thinking. It will make the injury easier for you to live with, and build a habit of good, positive thoughts. Does that make sense?"

I thought about it for a moment. "Yes. I can decide what I think about the injury, and that'll make it easier for me to live with it."

"That's right. The more positive, hopeful, and clear your thoughts are, the happier you'll be. You can put the thoughts you need in your mind, thoughts like 'I will think positive.' You decide what you want to think, and good thinking helps improve your life."

"How do I create the thoughts to make my injury more comfortable?"

"You keep thinking and praying about it, and the answers will come to you."

I turned the oyster story over in my mind and realized that everyone had irritants in their life, and that we can choose how to respond to them, and our choices shape our life. I wanted to make only good choices.

I DIDN'T DRIVE much, but occasionally I ran errands alone. I tried to remember to use a list when I went grocery shopping, but I usually forgot.

One day, when I returned home from shopping, Tom asked, "Darling, did you buy the light bulb?"

I looked up from putting away the groceries. "What light bulb?"

Tom sighed. "The one for the lamp."

"Which lamp?"

"Mary, the lamp beside the living room couch, the one that needs a new bulb."

"You never said that lamp needs a new bulb."

"Yes, I did. You know it does. We've talked about it several times."

I shook my head. "No, we haven't."

"Yes, darling, we have. You've tried that lamp yourself. I keep asking you to remember to buy the bulb, and you keep saying you will, but you forget. Please remember to buy it the next time you go to the store."

I shrugged. "Okay."

"You need to keep working to remember things. It's hard on both of us when you don't. The light bulb is a good chance to practice strengthening your memory. And I keep reminding you to write things down. You need to remember to use a list."

"Yes, dear."

A few days later, I drove to the grocery to get a few things, and this time, I remembered to bring a list. I gathered everything and then, as I was getting ready to check out, I realized I'd forgotten to put something on the list.

It tugged at my mind—*ahh, I need a light bulb!*

I smiled at myself. I'd remembered. Another victory.

50

Dancing

Since my accident, I had only seen everything as black or white, right or wrong—with nothing in between. But now, I realized I needed to open my mind, to view things with a broader understanding.

Gradually, I began noticing more shades of gray in everyday situations—subtle differences I'd previously missed. I was getting better at detecting these nuances, but it wasn't easy. I had to accept that not everything fit into a simple category that was easily defined. But little by little, I learned to embrace the complexity.

Another lesson I learned was that not every problem was a crisis. For a long time, I had believed every issue needed an instant answer. I'd react first and think later. But gradually, I realized that some things were better left to simmer; not everything required an instant resolution. Some issues, I found, were better addressed with patience, or even postponed until a later time. And I realized that not all problems were of equal importance, which helped me see things more clearly. I learned it was best to look at situations on a case-by-case basis, and I began to measure things on a sliding scale. That helped me immensely. Some things mattered deeply, while others could be set aside without guilt or worry. With this new understanding, I became less concerned about little things. I learned to breathe easier, and to live more freely.

I discovered it was essential to maintain a positive mental attitude. When life dealt me a bad hand of cards, I couldn't just throw them on the table and say, "I'm not playing that hand; I want a new one." Life didn't work that way. Instead, I had to face each problem head-on, apply myself, and work to solve it. I understood now that staying positive, even in the face of adversity, would help me live the best life.

As I reflected on everything I had been through—my mistakes, trials, and heartaches—I realized that my Christian faith remained unbroken. Faith swept away doubt, gave me strength, and reminded me that, no matter what, I was not alone.

I shared these thoughts with Tom one evening, and he took my hands in his. "Lord, thank you for being my Lord, and Mary's. Thank you for forgiving our mistakes. Thank you for your presence in our lives. Thank you for your Word that guides us. Help us seek your will in everything. Please bless us with your protection. Amen."

Then he read a scripture to me: "Be kind and compassionate to one another, forgiving each other, just as in Christ God forgave you."[10]

---

[10] Ephesians 4:32

As I listened, I realized how vital grace and forgiveness were, in all relationships. I thought about how often I had failed, how often I had made mistakes, yet Tom never held them against me. He forgave me again and again. No matter how many times I faltered, he was there, lifting me up, showing me love.

Tom found another scripture he liked, and read it: "God is our refuge and strength, an ever-present help in trouble."[11]

That scripture resonated inside me. It had been very true in the aftermath of my accident.

It was a blessing Tom and I already had a strong faith in God before the accident happened. That faith had been the bedrock of my recovery, and was a strength we always drew on.

THE NEXT MORNING, Tom woke me up with, "Good morning, darling. I have something for you."

I sat up, surprised, and he placed a tray on my lap—coffee, eggs, and toast. I smiled up at him. "What did I do to deserve this?"

He smiled back. "You don't have to do anything. You're special to me, and I want you to know how important you are."

Tears welled up in my eyes.

I love you," he said.

"I love you too," I whispered back, my heart full. In that moment, with his love surrounding me, I felt completely understood.

---

[11] Psalm 46:1

AS TIME PASSED, life became more and more fun.

Tom signed us up for ballroom dancing lessons. We started with two left feet, stumbling and stepping on each other's toes, and we laughed together all around the dance floor. Learning the dance steps was hard, but we practiced over and over, enjoying every moment.

One day as we practiced, a memory suddenly surfaced. "Tom," I said, as he guided me into a turn, "I remember we used to go out dancing at King's Table."

His eyebrows rose, and he smiled. "That's right. We used to dance to almost every song. Those were some good times."

I continued counting the beats of the music, moving my feet with each count. "I remember," I said, as he led me into another turn.

He smiled, a glint of pride in his eyes. "That was a long time ago. Good for you for remembering."

We practiced the new dance steps again and again, gradually getting better. And that's exactly what recovering from a brain injury is like—learning the new steps of life. At first, it's hard, and there's stumbling along the way, but the end result is worth it. Having another turn around the dance floor of life is truly rewarding.

51

Every Day is a Gift

Eight Years After

The phrase "Every day is a gift" had become very meaningful to us. We were intensely aware that life could be over in a single moment.

Before my accident, I believed my life was too good for tragedy to find me. I'd naively thought I was somehow protected from the kind of disaster that happened to *other* people. But the accident shattered that illusion. It taught me that life is unpredictable, that a problem could come out of nowhere. I'd learned intimately how uncertain life is. It could turn on a dime and be over in the blink of an eye. I carried that awareness with me every day, and it shaped the way I lived. I knew that everyone was only a single breath away from death—and knowing it made each moment infinitely more precious.

I would never look at life the same way as before. Tomorrow isn't guaranteed. Life was fragile, and every day should be treasured. I became determined to live each day as if it were my last and to not waste a single second.

I WAS STILL seeing a counselor once a month, and during my next visit, I shared my thoughts about the unpredictability of life. As I spoke, the counselor nodded, her eyes thoughtful. Then she told me that my recovery had been very good, and that I'd reached the point where I no longer needed counseling. I hadn't considered counseling would stop, but as her words sank in, a sense of peace and satisfaction washed through me. I had come so far, and I realized that a chapter in my healing was complete.

When I shared the news with Tom, his face lit up. He pulled me close, hugging me tight.

"I'm so proud of you, Mary. You've made a lot of recovery. It wasn't easy, but you did it."

"We did it together, Tom." My heart was filled with happiness. "I couldn't have done it without you."

He smiled and kissed my cheek. "Darling, I love you. You're the joy of my life, and I would do anything for you."

I reached up and touched the necklace he'd given me so many years before and felt blessed.

TOM AND I realized that I needed to start making more decisions. Since the accident, I'd relied on him to make them, but now, I needed to strengthen my ability. It was a gradual process, that unfolded with choices I began to make each day.

I started driving more often by myself, each turn of the wheel strengthening my sense of independence. Grocery shopping by myself was still challenging, but I embraced it with more determination, and I discovered it wasn't as hard as I'd thought. But it was when I began clothes shopping on my own that I realized something unexpected: I really enjoyed it. Gradually, I kept becoming more confident and more able to stand on my own two feet.

During one of my shopping trips, I decided to buy Tom a special gift. I found a jewelry store that sold pocket watches and bought a gold one. I had the store engrave a message on the inside cover, something that expressed my feelings for him. Later that day, I returned to pick up the watch. I opened the cover and read the inscription:

"Tom, Every day spent with you is a gift. Love, Mary."

It was perfect. As I slipped the box containing the watch into my purse, a giddy rush of excitement surged through me—I couldn't wait to give it to him.

The next morning, Sunday, we attended church. As we walked in, energy buzzed in the air. The sanctuary lights had been dimmed, and soft music played. The lyrics of the opening song appeared on a screen at the front, and the congregation began to sing. It felt invigorating.

I enjoyed my ability to hear each individual part of the music, the layers of harmony weaving together. Tom smiled and asked me to softly sing the part for the soprano, then the alto, then the tenor. It amused him that I could hear each one. Then we sang his tenor part together.

When the music ended, the lights came up, and the pastor delivered an inspiring message of love and hope.

A deep peace settled over me. I remembered how important church membership had been to me. It was a part of my life that had gotten lost.

But now, I knew in my heart that I wanted to belong to a church family again. I couldn't wait to tell Tom how I felt.

At the end of the service, we joined the church.

Afterward, as we walked to the car, Tom said, "Mary, I think we should go out to lunch and celebrate joining the church. Would you like to drive?"

"That sounds great," I said.

I unzipped my purse to get my keys and that's when I saw it—*Tom's watch!* I'd forgotten to give it to him.

At the restaurant, after we ordered, I smiled at Tom and said, "I love you, sweetheart, and I have a present for you."

His eyes widened. "What?"

I handed him the box, watching as he carefully opened it and looked at the watch.

"Oh, Mary, this is beautiful!" He opened the cover and read the inscription. "Wow, I love the message! Thank you."

His reaction filled me with joy, my heart soaring in a way that only love can make someone feel. In that moment, I knew that the new decisions I'd begun to make, the growth I'd started to find within myself, were all part of something much bigger—a shared life with Tom, built on love.

WE BEGAN ATTENDING Sunday morning church service regularly. Soon we joined a Sunday school class. Not long after that, we joined the choir.

I loved singing in the choir. Tom, on the other hand, didn't enjoy choir as much as I did, but he stayed by my side, supporting me all the same. We got in the routine of attending Wednesday night choir practice together, enjoying the shared experience.

Weeks passed, and gradually, I gained the confidence to attend choir practice on my own. Tom chose to attend a Bible study instead, so he was still close by, yet I found myself navigating this time on my own, with Tom's support.

I shared my testimony with the choir, describing the experience of my head injury. Until that moment, I had kept it mostly to myself, Tom, doctors, counselors, and other survivors. Speaking about it felt freeing, like a weight was lifted from my shoulders. The support of the choir members was wonderful, their kindness and understanding wrapping around me like a warm embrace.

Having a church family was an answer I hadn't even known was missing. It gave me a deep sense of belonging.

I began to think how life was like a giant puzzle with lots of pieces. Some fit together, some didn't. Deciphering the puzzle pieces and their connections was important to me. I was sure that going to church and being in the choir were puzzle pieces that fit.

A FEW WEEKS later, I met one of my girlfriends from choir at the mall for a little shopping. We talked, laughed, and had a blast.

When we said goodbye, I walked out of the mall and headed to the car. But in the parking lot, I realized it was missing. I walked all over the lot, thinking I'd forgotten where I'd parked, but it was nowhere to be found.

Finally, I gave up and called the police. "I need to report a stolen car."

Two officers came and met with me. As we stood among the parked vehicles, I described the car. One officer started writing on a little notepad. Then he looked at me and said, "Ma'am, do you have someone who can come pick you up?"

"Yes," I said. I called Tom and said, "You're not going to believe what happened."

"Darling, are you okay?" he asked with concern.

"Yes, yes. But someone's stolen the car."

"What? Not our brand-new car?"

"Oh!" My hand flew to my mouth as realization hit me—we'd traded in our old car and gotten a new one. Then I saw it right behind the officer who stood in front of me, listening to my call. Our new car was right there.

"You're right," I said, relief flooding through me. "I've got to go." I hung up.

Embarrassed, I explained to the officers that I'd forgotten we had traded in the old car for a new one. Two steps forward, one step back—that's how it felt in that moment.

The officers were kind, their smiles easing some of my embarrassment. "It's a simple mistake," one of them said.

"You're good, then?" the other one asked.

I nodded, still a bit flustered. But that was better than if the car had been stolen.

As I drove home, memories of my car accident and near-death experience suddenly shot through me. I remembered walking into the bright light and seeing my dad and Jesus standing there, and the feeling of love and peace I'd felt.

I recalled the conversation:

"Daddy, I'm coming to be with you."

"You can't, Mary. It's not your time."

"But I want to be here."

"No, not until the time is right."

I looked at Jesus. "I want to be in heaven."

He answered, "Remember these words: 'I will not die but live, and will proclaim what the Lord has done.'"[12]

Wow! I'd finally remembered the words Jesus had spoken to me!

Remembering that moment felt like a light turning on inside my mind. I'd tried so many times to recall Jesus's words, and now, I finally had.

The realization thrilled me.

I didn't know why the memory surfaced just then, on that quiet drive home, but that was how my brain worked—like it had a mind of its own.

The minute I walked through the door, I told Tom what Jesus had said to me.

He wrapped me in a hug.

---

[12] Psalm 118:17

"That's wonderful, Mary. I'm glad you finally remembered it. Do you understand what it means?"

I had tried to figure it out, but couldn't. "No."

Tom drew me closer. "Well, Jesus said you will, so just give it time."

52

Poetry

One afternoon, I found a box of books that remained untouched since our move. I took each one out and placed it on a shelf in the living room. At the bottom of the box, I saw a three-ring binder, its cover labeled simply, "Mary's Poetry." A wave of nostalgia washed over me. I had loved writing poems before the accident, and hadn't thought about it after that.

I opened the binder, and with each page I turned, memories of writing the poems flooded back. It was like reconnecting with a part of myself I had lost.

I placed the binder on the shelf and sat down at the kitchen table, pencil in hand, a fresh sheet of paper before me. As I reflected on my life, and the struggles I'd had since the accident, I felt a stirring within me.

But more than the struggles, I began to think about the source of my hope and strength: my relationship with God. He carried me through the darkest of times, and I couldn't imagine a life without him.

Gratitude filled my heart, and with it, the words began to flow, one after another, like a stream of thoughts seeking release.

When I finished, I showed my new poem to Tom. He read it silently, a smile spreading across his face. "It's beautiful," he said, his voice warm with encouragement. "You should write more."

I read the poem again:

When the Mountain Seems Too High

When the mountain seems too high to climb,
And you think it's something you can't do,
Remember God's promise in His Word,
Not to ask something too hard for you.

When the path is dimly lighted,
And you can't find your place,
Just trust in God for His support,
And He will lead you with His grace.

He will never leave your side,
Even when you feel alone,
He's always there to guide you,
And help you get back home.

When you want to give up,
Look to Him, He will be there,
Ready to lend a helping hand,
And take away your fear.

Trust in God for strength,
He will see you through,
With God on your side,
There is nothing you can't do.

So reach out in faith,
He's there to take your hand,
He will get you through the storm,
And plant your feet back on dry land.

Mary Parker
2-6-2009

53

New Beginnings

Nine Years After

As I reflected on Mary and her TBI, it became clear to me that I had loved two versions of the same woman: the Mary before the accident, and the Mary after it. They were, in many ways, two distinctly different people. The Mary I knew now was a blend of who she had once been and who she had become, and understanding this made my life much easier.

ONE EVENING, I walked into our bedroom while Mary was getting ready for one of our dinner dates. The soft fragrance of her perfume hung in the air.

"Hey, I know that scent," I said. "That's 'Beautiful,' isn't it?"

She crossed the room and wrapped her arms around my neck. "Yes, and I hope you always think I'm beautiful."

I pulled her close and kissed her gently. "I do."

She stepped back, her deep brown eyes bright with a smile. "You know how you're always telling me to write things down?"

"Yes," I said, curious where this was headed.

She reached for a sheet of paper lying on her dresser. "This is for you." She placed it in my hands.

Dear Tom,

There are no words to say how happy I am to be married to you. You are my Prince Charming. The way you cared for me after my accident was nothing short of amazing. You never gave up or made me feel that I was a burden. I can never tell you enough how very special you are and how blessed I am to have you as my husband.

I'm sure there were times when you felt like throwing your hands up and saying "I quit" but you never did, and I applaud you. I have more respect for you than you will ever know.

You took a person's life that was broken into a million pieces and carefully and lovingly helped put it back together again. You are my hero. I know you would never say that about yourself, but it's true.

The injury opened the door for me to fall in love with you a second time, and I will always be thankful for that. Sharing my life with you has made the valleys less deep and the mountaintops much more beautiful. Now, after everything we've been through, here we are, falling in love again, and I want it to last forever.

You helped me in ways I may never know, but God does. Your rewards will be much greater in heaven.

I'm so thankful for you, your love, devotion, and Christian faith, and I'm proud of you. You have my heart. There's no way I could ever tell you how much I love you, and I will love you every day for the rest of my life.

Love, Mary

"DARLING," TOM SAID as he walked into the living room, "it's been almost ten years since the accident, and I think it's time for you to get back in front of the church and sing a solo again."

I looked up from my book, surprised. "Tom, I'm not sure I can."

"You're a wonderful singer," he said, his voice full of conviction. "You've been singing your whole life, and I know you can do it."

Could I?

The thought stopped me. I hadn't even *considered* singing a solo since the accident. Yet the idea intrigued me. From the time I was a little girl, I had sung solos in church. I loved it. People often told me I had a strong, clear voice—something

I always believed was a gift from God. Singing had been my way of sharing what Christ had done in my life, a way to give him glory. The accident had silenced that part of me, but now, I realized I had more reason than ever to sing my thanks.

After much discussion and prayer, I chose a song. Tom and I listened to it and sang it repeatedly, trying to imprint the music and words firmly into my memory. I sang it to him, he sang it to me, and we sang it together, over and over. After three months of steady practice, I finally felt ready. With a mix of excitement and nervousness, I contacted the church's choir director and scheduled my solo.

On the Sunday morning when I was to sing, I felt surprisingly confident. Tom and I arrived at church early and took our seats in the front pew. The service began with a speaker making the usual announcements, and then I was introduced. I stood, walked to the podium, and lifted the microphone. Looking up, I saw the sanctuary was packed—hundreds of people, and all their eyes were on me.

I felt swelling excitement as the music began to play. I waited for the moment I was supposed to start singing, and then—*nothing.*

All the words that were familiar just moments before had vanished from my memory.

What do I do now? I can't just walk off the stage. I've got to do something.

The music played on, and I closed my eyes.

Lord, I don't know what the words are, but I'm going to open my mouth, and you put whatever words you want me to sing in there, and let it bring honor to you.

I opened my eyes, waited for the music to come back to the right place, and started to sing. I didn't question what the words were—I just sang my heart out, feeling the music, enjoying the moment.

When I finished, the congregation erupted in a standing ovation. My heart overflowed with joy.

After the service, the pastor came up to me and said, "I've never heard that version of that song before."

"And you never will again," I replied with a smile. The truth was, I had no idea what I'd actually sung.

As we walked out of the church, Tom said, "I was watching and praying for you, but when the moment came for you to sing, you closed your eyes instead, and then you sang those different words. What happened?"

I told him everything, and when I finished, he nodded thoughtfully and smiled. "Do you know what probably just happened?"

"What?"

"You blessed someone with that song—with those words. Someone heard exactly what they needed to hear."

"You really think so?" I asked.

"Yes, I do."

I felt a warmth rise inside me. His words drew my attention to a powerful truth. I may not be able to do something, but God can do anything. And when we place our trust in him, everything goes according to plan—God's plan.

AT MARY'S ANNUAL check-up with Dr. Anderson, he asked her how she'd been doing since her last visit.

She said proudly, "Well, I haven't had any falls in the last year."

His eyebrows lifted above his glasses. "That's excellent news."

He went through her exam methodically, as always, testing everything. "Mary, you're doing good. You don't need to see me again until your next annual check-up, unless something comes up."

We walked out of his office happy about her progress. It had taken her nearly ten years to be able to walk again without falling, but it had finally happened, and it was a huge relief to us.

I LOOKED THROUGH a photo album that contained pictures of Cody and Beth's wedding, the past smiling at me. I lingered on each photo, feeling a quiet ache in my chest, and wished I could remember my own wedding. Not as fragments, but as something I could *feel* again.

I told Tom what was on my heart, and he looked at me with a warm smile and said, almost casually, "Why don't we have a ceremony to renew our wedding vows?"

The words landed like a spark. "How would we do that?"

"We could take a cruise," he said, "and renew our vows during it. We can have the ceremony at the start of the cruise, and then"—his smile widened—"the rest of the cruise can be a honeymoon."

In that instant, everything aligned. The wedding I couldn't remember was replaced by a future I could choose. Not a redo, but something even better: a celebration written on our own terms.

We chose a Caribbean cruise with Celebrity Cruises. As the departure date approached, excitement filled us. This wasn't just a vacation—it was a love story reclaimed. A new beginning wrapped in sunlight, ocean air, and open horizons.

I was thrilled by what was coming next.

MARY SQUEEZED MY hand as we crossed the walkway onto the cruise ship. A light breeze lifted her hair from her forehead, and when she looked at me her eyes were shining with excitement.

"I can't believe we're really here," she said, laughing. "I'm so happy we're doing this."

I felt that same joy well up inside me. The ship, sleek and gleaming under the sun, buzzed with energy—music, laughter, and animated voices filling the air. We threaded our way through the crowd and down a narrow corridor lined with cabin doors until we found ours. We stepped inside and checked it out. Every inch was designed for comfort, and we laughed as we began to settle in.

Then the ship shifted gently and began to pull away from the pier.

We opened the sliding glass door and stepped onto our private balcony. People waved from the shore, growing smaller by the second, and we waved back, grinning like kids.

Our adventure stretched ahead, and a thrill shot straight through me. We were really doing this. There was no going back—only forward on the ocean.

A few minutes later, Mary started unpacking while I headed off to find the ship's chaplain to finalize our ceremony. Somewhere aboard this ship, we would stand together and say our vows again, on our second day at sea.

Then Mary and I set out to explore the ship. Every turn revealed something new and dazzling. Glittering shops, casual fast-food spots, elegant restaurants, a casino, and more. The ship felt endless, alive, and like a world unto itself. Eventually, we claimed lounge chairs near one of the pools, and a waitress delivered slices of hot pizza and cold drinks.

We leaned back, ate, laughed, and let it all sink in. We weren't just passengers on a cruise ship—we were riding a wave of joy, anticipation, and second chances.

I taught Mary how to play shuffleboard, joking it was an important skill for our retirement years. It made us laugh.

The next morning, I stepped out of the cabin to confirm some final details with the chaplain. We settled on noon for the ceremony. Back in the cabin, Mary and I dressed for the occasion—Hawaiian shirts, colorful shorts, and deck shoes.

We met the chaplain in the ship's chapel, an elegant, cozy space. The moment we stepped inside, I couldn't help but notice the contrast between our bright, colorful resort wear and his crisp white uniform, gold stripes gleaming on his shoulders. Mary and I shared a knowing glance between us, chuckling softly.

Looking radiant, Mary beamed at me, and the rest of the world melted away, leaving only the two of us and the promise we were making again. My ideas didn't always hit the mark, but this one had been a home run.

As the chaplain guided us through the brief ceremony, I realized how perfectly the term "vow renewal" fit what we were doing. This wasn't a rerun of our wedding day; it was a declaration that our love had evolved, deepened, and grown stronger with time, and with each word we spoke, we were renewing our love and our lives. The bond between us was more solid than ever. We weren't the same people who had stood at the altar so long ago—life had changed us, and now, we were embracing that change. In that intimate chapel, with the gentle sway of the ship beneath our feet, our love felt alive, renewed, and limitless.

AS I SAID, "I do," Tom grinned, and a wave of excitement swept through me, as if I were marrying him for the first time. And in a way, I was, since the old Mary was gone, replaced by the new Mary, shaped by all I had become since the accident.

When the chaplain pronounced us husband and wife, Tom drew me into his arms and kissed me, and a joyful feeling flooded me. As we walked out of the chapel, hand in hand, heading to the sunny top deck, I tried to press the memories deeply into my mind, wanting to always remember them.

The band playing by the pool serenaded us as gentle breezes blew, and we danced and laughed, wrapped up in each other and the joy of the moment.

AS WE WALKED back to our cabin, Mary's eyes sparkled in the warm afternoon sunlight. I'd worried the day's excitement might tire her, but she seemed quietly energized, a soft smile lighting her face.

On our balcony, we shared a seafood dinner and watched the sun sink toward the horizon. After the meal, as the ship glided onward with a faint, gentle rocking motion and soft creaking sounds, we lingered together on the balcony, enjoying each other's company.

"I'm so happy, Tom," Mary said, her voice warm.

"I am too, darling. It's been a perfect day, and you're the perfect bride."

She looked down, then back up at me, her eyes luminous. "My love for you is deeper than the ocean," she murmured.

"Sweetheart, that was a beautiful thing to say. I love you too."

She smiled, reaching across the table for my hand, and I felt her wedding ring, a small symbol for a big love.

ON OUR HONEYMOON in the middle of the Caribbean, Tom and I were starting over, and happiness filled my heart. My love for him was stronger than I ever remembered, and I hoped that the joy I felt would always stay with me. As we cruised across the ocean, I knew that no matter where life took us, we had each other, for better or worse.

Lord, thank you for second chances. I'm not sure how you orchestrated my life in such a way to bring Tom and me together, but I'm sure glad you did. I am so thankful for his love. Thank you, Lord, for your hand in my life.

54

Living with Joy

One day, as I had done many times before, I picked up my Bible and started to read. I stopped in astonishment, then reread the words I saw: "I will not die but live, and will proclaim what the Lord has done."[13]

Those were the very words Jesus had spoken to me in my near-death experience—in the bright light at the end of the hallway. And now here they were again, printed in black and white right in front of me.

In that instant, I understood the meaning behind what Jesus had said to me: I was supposed to tell the story of what he had done in my life.

I turned to Tom and said, "We need to write a book about our experience." I explained everything that had just become clear to me, and he listened with quiet understanding, nodding without hesitation.

---

[13] Psalm 118:17

And that is how this memoir came to be. In these pages, we share the miracle of how Jesus carried us through the injury and the recovery.

Some people think the miracles of Jesus ended long ago, but I know firsthand that isn't true. Every day, when I look in the mirror, I see a miracle looking back at me—a reminder of God's love, and the life that continues because of it.

God has been so good to me. He saved me, healed me, and blessed me far beyond what anyone could have imagined. He protected me from the brink of death, both during the accident and afterward, when the doctor had to shock my heart three times to restart it. With God's grace, I recovered from a devastating injury more fully than anyone expected. The odds were against me, yet I serve an unchanging God who defies all odds. I am eternally grateful for his love, and I will continually give him the glory for everything he has done. He chose to heal me, and in response, I choose to walk in the light of his love.

Praise God for his unfailing love, his goodness, and his miraculous power!

Thank you, Lord, for being my Lord and for everything you have done for me. Thank you for my amazing recovery and for the joy I have. You've blessed me in ways I can't comprehend. I'm grateful for all that you have done in my life. I don't understand the depth of your love, but I am so thankful for it. Lord, what a wonderful God you are! I will always try my best to be the person you want me to be, and I ask for your forgiveness where I fall short. Please continue to guide me as I seek your will and your wisdom. Amen.

55

Brighter Days Ahead

Ten Years After

As I look back on the long, winding road I've traveled, I see not just what I've endured, but the person I've become. I remember the early years of my recovery, when the darkness of the brain injury was terrifying—everything was unknown. But moving through the darkness and into the light again was renewing. It feels as though I've been reborn, and I see everything with a new vision. Although I'm different from the person I was before, I embrace who I've become.

Having a brain injury is like being a member of a club you don't want to belong to but having no choice about it. Membership means being on a ride you don't want to be on, and you can't get off the ride, but you *can* decide your attitude. There are times when I don't like the truth, but I can't change it, so I choose to accept it, stay positive, and keep moving forward.

I have accepted that my brain injury will always be a part of me, and I'll always have extra challenges due to it, but the gift of being alive is far too precious to waste on worrying about what I cannot change.

My faith in God has been essential in my life. Never was I more aware of how much I needed him than after my accident. When a problem occurs, especially a big one, it's best to already be walking closely with God, leaning on his strength and guidance every step of the way.

Brain injury isn't an easy path, but with determination, faith in God, and the support of caring people, I endured it, regained lost abilities, and started over. I have a satisfying and fulfilling life, full of love, and although I have a brain injury, the injury doesn't have me.

The lighthearted contentment of everyday life has returned. My mind is calm, and my heart overflows with joy. I've discovered a new ability to make choices, to decide the direction of my life and how to live it. I choose to move toward truth, love, and knowledge, and to have good relationships with God, my husband, and others who care about me. Every day, I am grateful for the time I still have to live, and I am determined to make the best decisions I can. I am hopeful and excited for what the future holds.

My husband and I are deeply in love, and our marriage is good. My mom, half of my siblings, and two of my three children became estranged from me after the accident because they couldn't reconcile the old Mary with the new one, but now, thankfully, those relationships are mostly improving. Mom and I have grown closer, and some of my siblings have come back into my life. Dylan has shown signs of wanting to reconnect, through occasional phone calls and texting. Cody is still distant, for now. Hopefully, the two younger children will find their way back to a closer family relationship. Leo has stayed close. I cherish the love of those who walk beside me, who never let me face life's storms alone.

I am thankful that my dear Tom never wavered during the biggest challenge of our lives. When my world turned upside down, he was my anchor—steadfast, devoted, and willing to be my hero. His love was instrumental in my recovery, and I hope our story inspires others to step into the role of hero as well.

I am completely at peace with the new person I've become. I'm different now, reshaped by my journey, yet still a child of God and a woman of faith, learning to live each day with courage, grace, and hard-won joy.

RIGHT AFTER MARY'S accident, the doctors told me that the most recovery from a TBI happened in the first few years. If Mary and I had believed that, she might not have recovered as fully as she has. Our experience is proof that the path of recovery unfolds unpredictably.

Mary thinks differently now than she did before the accident. Her perspective is unusual, and she still hangs our clothes on hangers that match the color of the clothing. But her attitude is optimistic, and so is mine.

Far more than a positive attitude, it's our faith in God that powers our lives. In both easy times and difficult ones, we can't imagine living without it. We trust God to help us in everything.

If you or someone you know has suffered a TBI, don't give up. Whether you are a survivor, a caregiver, a family member, or anyone else, you are not alone. Life may not return to what it once was, but there is always hope to find a new normal with peace and happiness.

We hope that sharing our story has been helpful. We survived a major life-changing event, and you can too, with brighter days ahead.

Acknowledgments

We are grateful for all the help we received from others after the car accident, especially Dr. Strider for his wise insight into traumatic brain injury and his advice, and for those who assisted us in producing this book.

Scripture References

These scriptures were very helpful as we worked to recover from traumatic brain injury.

I can do all this through him who gives me strength.
—Philippians 4:13

With God all things are possible.
—Matthew 19:26

Cast your cares on the Lord and he will sustain you.
—Psalm 55:22

Your word is a lamp for my feet, a light on my path.
—Psalm 119:105

Do not be anxious about anything, but in every situation, by prayer and petition, with thanksgiving, present your requests to God.
—Philippians 4:6

Trust in the Lord with all your heart.
—Proverbs 3:5

Commit to the Lord whatever you do, and he will establish your plans.
—Proverbs 16:3

If God is for us, who can be against us?
—Romans 8:31

Whatever is true, whatever is noble, whatever is right, whatever is pure, whatever is lovely, whatever is admirable—if anything is excellent or praiseworthy—think about such things.
—Philippians 4:8

God is our refuge and strength, an ever-present help in trouble.
—Psalm 46:1

Be kind and compassionate to one another, forgiving each other, just as in Christ God forgave you.
—Ephesians 4:32

I will not die but live, and will proclaim what the Lord has done.
—Psalm 118:17

www.ingramcontent.com/pod-product-compliance
Lightning Source LLC
LaVergne TN
LVHW011320080426
835513LV00006B/137